Praise for Stoned Again

"Mike Sager is a journalistic icon and a literary force. A whole generation of writers has been shaped and guided by his work. This is a seminal collection by a master of the form."

—Wil S. Hylton, *New York Times Magazine* contributor, author of *Vanished: The Sixty-Year Search for the Missing Men of World War II*

"In *Stoned Again*, Mike Sager refers to himself as a 'drugs correspondent,' but that's legitimately humble smoke that belies what's really going on here. While there's plenty of weed, heroin, shrooms, and crack (not to mention plenty of Ricky James, bitch) in these pages, what is most evident on every page is the remarkable reporting, empathy, craftsmanship, and storytelling that have rightly placed Mike Sager among the journalistic legends of our time."

—Maximillian Potter, author of *Shadows in the Vineyard: The True Story of the Plot to Poison the World's Greatest Wine*

"An entertaining and absorbing collection from a leading voice on drugs in America."

—Nushin Rashidian, co-author of *A New Leaf: The End of Cannabis Prohibition*

"Sager's belief that marijuana expands one's perceptions mirrors my own experiences and beliefs. If you are a marijuana smoker, you'll find this book a good read."

—Keith Stroup, founder of NORML, the National Organization for the Reform of Marijuana Laws

Praise for Mike Sager

"Like his journalistic precursors Tom Wolfe and Hunter S. Thompson, Sager writes frenetic, off-kilter pop-sociological profiles of Americans in all their vulgarity and vitality. He writes with flair, but only in the service of an omnivorous curiosity. He defies expectations in pieces that lesser writers would play for satire or sensationalism . . . a Whitmanesque ode to teeming humanity's mystical unity."

—*The New York Times Book Review*

"Mike Sager writes about places and events we seldom get a look at — and people from whom we avert our eyes. But with Sager in command of all the telling details, he shows us history, humanity, humor, sometimes even honor. He makes us glad to live with our eyes wide open."

—Richard Ben Cramer, Pulitzer Prize winning author of *What It Takes: The Way to the White House* and *Joe Dimaggio: The Hero's Life*

"Nobody alive today is writing better long magazine pieces than Mike Sager. If you want to find out what the gold standard looks like, or if you just want to read a breathtaking portrait of our motley nation, buy this book."

—Kurt Andersen, author, *True Believers*, host of *Studio 360*

"Like a silver-tongued Margaret Mead, Sager slips into foreign societies almost unnoticed and lives among the natives, chronicling his observations in riveting long-form narratives that recall a less tragic, less self-involved Hunter S. Thompson and a more relatable Tom Wolfe."

—*Performances*

"Mike Sager is the Beat poet of American journalism, that rare reporter who can make literature out of shabby reality. Equal parts reporter, ethnographer, stylist and cultural critic, Sager has for 20 years carried the tradition of Tom Wolfe on his broad shoulders, chronicling the American scene and psyche. Nobody does it sharper, smarter, or with more style."

—Walt Harrington, author of *Acts of Creation*, journalism professor, University of Illinois at Urbana-Champaign

"I can recognize the truth in these stories—tales about the darkest possible side of wretched humanity. Sager has obviously spent too much time in flop houses in Laurel Canyon."

— Hunter S. Thompson, author of *Fear and Loathing in Las Vegas* and *Hells Angels*

Other books by Mike Sager

High Tolerance, A Novel

The Someone You're Not

Scary Monsters and Super Freaks

Revenge of the Donut Boys

Wounded Warriors

Deviant Behavior, A Novel

The Devil and John Holmes

BYLINER SELECTS

Stoned Again

The High Times and Strange Life of a Drugs Correspondent

MIKE SAGER

STONED AGAIN: The High Times and Strange Life of a Drugs Correspondent | Mike Sager

Published in the United States of America.
Cataloging-in-Publication data for this book is available from the Library of Congress.

ISBN-13: 978-0-9862679-7-0
ISBN-10: 098626797X

Cover illustrated by Brett Whaley
Cover Designed by Stravinski Pierre and Siori Kitajima, SF AppWorks
http://sfappworks.com
Formatting by Ovidiu Vlad, SF AppWorks LLC.
Published by The Sager Group
info@TheSagerGroup.net
info@MikeSager.com

BYLINER SELECTS

Stoned Again

The High Times and Strange Life of a Drugs Correspondent

MIKE SAGER

Editor's Note

This book was originally created in eBook form by Byliner Selects/Vook

For Gloria

黃雯頌

Table of Contents

Introduction

A man (or a woman) on a mission to score drugs is never a tourist, and neither is one who is passing a pipe.

As you will read in the first essay in this collection, "When Should a Man Stop Smoking Weed?", I have smoked pot with a variety of people over the years, including "gangbangers, actors, rap stars, construction workers, bankers, homeless guys and millionaires. I've smoked at 14,000 feet in the Nepalese Himalayas with a Sherpa guide; at 36,000 feet in a commercial airliner back in the days when they had smoking sections; at just below sea level on the beach of Marlon Brando's private atoll with a topless Tahitian translator; in the ruins of a factory in North Philadelphia with a bunch of 13-year-olds while watching pit bulls fight to the death—hey, all of those kids worked shifts selling cocaine and had juvie records a mile long."

You could probably substitute the words "drunk alcohol with" and come up with a pretty good story as well, though you might not remember as many of the details. But the point is this: As the ideologues of the Just Say No movement have been fond of trumpeting, marijuana has indeed been a gateway for me.

Smoking pot has opened the doors of my perception. It has led to meetings with new kinds of people outside my home community, ethnicity, religion or economic station, people of like minds from different places. It has led me to the understanding that a person can find communality with any other human, in any setting, no matter how scary or how different they might seem.

I haven't smoked pot with *all* the people I've interviewed. I didn't smoke with the white supremacists from the Aryan

Nations, for instance, or with the high school boy from Orange County (until years later), or with Angelina Jolie—though I know a guy who used to sell pot to Brad Pitt a long time ago, when he was fond of Jennifer Aniston and delivery pizza.

But I have smoked with a good many people all over the world, and it has led to a simple conclusion that has informed every bit of the work I've done as a journalist: Deep down, people are just people. We are all the same and deserve to be treated with the same respect. Angelina, the six hundred pound man, the members of a crack gang from Venice, CA, even the Nazi-worshipping miscreants from the Aryan Nations.

Drugs have given me that insight.

And I even remembered it the next day.

And all the days that followed.

* * *

I smoked pot for the first time in 1968, when I was 12 years old and smoking pot was as much of a political act as a means of getting high—I didn't even know what being *high* was about at the time, it was an abstract concept, kind of like sex. I knew it would be good, but really, I had *no idea*.

I'd never been drunk, though I'd been allowed, liberally, to sip my parents' wine or scotch or crème de menthe. My parents were sober people who worked anxiously to maintain control in every aspect of life. My dad's big college drinking story involved a show-down with a rival frat member. My dad won by discreetly pouring his drinks into a potted plant.

For me, getting high that first time wasn't about getting high in the negative sense that we think of it today. It wasn't *abuse*. It was use. I wasn't trying to escape my desperate circumstances. I wasn't chasing sensual or thought-expanding experiences, though that may have become more of a goal at a later date. I wasn't trying to forget my problems; I didn't really have any. And I wasn't particularly trying to rebel against my parents, who were very good to me, though rebellion was a big part of the youth culture that was reshaping the landscape all around me.

It was the time of the Tet offensive in Vietnam; it was clear the war was becoming a lost cause. The anti-war, civil rights, and women's movements had begun to roil; President Lyndon Johnson had already delivered his surrender speech to the counter culture and the coming new age, announcing that he wouldn't run for a second term. *Hey Hey LBJ. How many kids did you kill today?* The status quo of the old white men was beginning to give way to the feelings and needs of the young, the female, and the disenfranchised.

At age 12, deciding to smoke pot—and going to some considerable effort to find some, and to figure out how to smoke it—was about two things. First, it signified I had joined the revolution my slightly older comrades, the baby boomers, had started. You grew your hair, starting with the forelock. You smoked pot. You bought your first pair of jeans, which weren't even allowed in school; in junior high we had a vitriolic protest to force the administration to legalize dungarees.

I smoked for the first time with my friend Boots Friedman and this weird kid he knew named Milton, whose parents, I could swear, were acting like Soviet spies. We sat outside behind the garage. It was summer in Baltimore, hot and sticky, the night songs of the cicadas in full chorus. I remember the sense that my perspective had changed. And that my head was floating. I felt like my face was on a balloon floating above my body, tethered by a string.

All across the country, similar initiation ceremonies were being carried out in groups of two and three, at camp sites, in basements, in Volkswagen Beetles with all the windows closed so as not to waste any smoke. "*Turn on, tune in, drop out,*" advised the acid guru Timothy Leary at the Human Be-In, a gathering of 30,000 hippies in San Francisco's Golden Gate Park in 1967. Later it was learned that phrase had been coined for him by philosopher Marshall McLuhan, the same guy who said "the medium is the message." Whoever was responsible, we young folk were hearing loud and clear. We were being urged to detach ourselves from existing conventions. To have sex, do drugs, be free. (Birth control pills were another wonderful new drug of this era.) You have to remember, the draft was hanging over every boy's head. Each night on the news, the war came to everyone's living room. Before it was over, in 1975, some 211,000 Americans were killed or wounded in Vietnam. They were all somebody's brother, the kid from the down the street. My next-door neighbor, with whom I played catch, tried to flee to Canada.

Maybe more important, at least in my own case, smoking pot was about pushing the boundaries of my sheltered suburban upbringing. With a long history of diaspora and persecution, my people, the Jews, tend to huddle together and create golden ghettos for themselves, which has worked out well in some cases but not so well in others. Moving to Pikesville, Maryland, my parents hoped to escape the persecution of their Southern upbringings. Yet, we transplanted Sagers always felt a sense of otherness, forever outsiders in this community with its strange and boisterous ways. The first person I ever heard utter the word *kike* was my mother. She'd been raised in a world a little like the one depicted in the movie *Driving Miss Daisy*. I guess you could say she believed in certain standards and practices that were quite different from the ones in operation in our adopted home town—which left me with a keen feeling that there was a lot more waiting to be found somewhere, and which fostered in me apparently an appetite for certain brands of deviant adventure.

* * *

I never set out to be a drugs correspondent.

That was the terminology used by Hunter S. Thompson, with whom I worked, at times closely, and then later succeeded in that unofficial/official position at *Rolling Stone*, and who I often think of in my own story as a personal Ghost of Christmas Future.

As I came of age as a journalist, in the late seventies and early eighties, the War on Drugs became a defining plank in the platform of our society. In a way you could say that my professional skills and my recreational expertise kind of dovetailed. I had a niche expertise.

Unlike many of the older, Ivy League Pollyannas sent by most news organizations to cover crime and drug-related stories—they seemed to mostly rely on the cops for their points of view—I had a lot of experience and insider information from the other side. By the time I got through college, I knew all about dealers and buys and stepping on shit to make more product to sell. Long before the crack epidemic, I learned how to cook freebase. Like a Harvard guy who majored in Chinese languages and became a decorated foreign correspondent, I spoke the language and customs of drugs, the dialects of the different exotic tribes within our national borders who dwelt in that world. And I was unafraid—because I already knew that people were just people, no matter how the media tried to portray them as the years went by.

As it happens, some of my fondest memories involve the subjects of these stories. Sleeper from the Venice Gang—he protected me from harm like a personal pit bull for every moment of my six weeks with his homies. I once stayed up all night convincing him not to kill someone who had ripped me off. As a favor to me, he let the guy live. Sleeper is dead now from AIDS, shared needles. Sometimes I drive by his ole lady's gramma's house. It's been redone and looks real fancy. I can still taste the hot tortillas slathered with butter that granny used to give us.

I'm an email or Facebook message away from Mark, Don, and David, who separately helped me enter the world of Generation H, young and artistic heroin addicts during the years of Max Fish and The Hat and the nineties hipster scene on the Lower East Side of Manhattan. Unfortunately, I find myself having to send David money every so often. He remains a genius, no matter how broken.

The Pope of Pot was a sweetheart, another mad genius—hmm, drugs seem to attract them. The Pope called everyone *toots*. A flamboyant gay man and amazing cockeyed optimist, he was fiercely unafraid to put his body on the line for the things he believed—and still have a good time doing it. He pissed off the cops and the New York City brass with his blatant protests and public sales of marijuana—he had the first delivery service in Manhattan, and said so openly. He called marijuana "the sacrament" and considered it a holy and healing plant. He even provided his crew of bicycle messengers with a dental plan. After radio's "King of All Media" Howard Stern got wind of the Pope's operation and called him live during a broadcast, the Pope eventually went to jail. Inside, he pissed blood for six months before he was allowed to see a doctor. With a fatal prognosis, the government let him go free. A few months later, he died of pancreatic cancer. He's memorialized as a character in my first novel, *Deviant Behavior.* I wonder what he would say if he knew that New York has now passed medical marijuana legislation.

A more recent acquaintance was Rick Ross—the real one, not the rapper—who I met for a story for *Esquire's* eightieth anniversary issue. Ross and I are near the same age with a similar look—aging athletic little guys, balding with a beard. Having reported on crack since the beginning, I'd crossed paths with Ross' work many times. I knew all the places, I knew the story, I knew all about him. Finally meeting him was like spending time with a significant historical figure—his part is critical to the understanding of the crack epidemic in this country. The story of the first time he saw cocaine and discovered the power of crack. Or the fact that it was Rick who taught the leaders of the Bloods and the Crips how to cook cocaine powder into crack, which led to the spread of the drug all over the country.

The closest and longest lasting relationship to come out of these stories was my friendship with Rick James.

I suppose our affinity was partly due to the fact that when I met him, and began writing about him for *Rolling Stone*, he was still in Folsom Prison, which was old and dank and not at all as cool as its image suggests. He had a girlfriend on the outside and some kids, but no real friends. I visited and wrote letters. I became his Boswell. That I (as a rep of a magazine) was paying attention to him and giving him respect, even in his abject condition, was important to him.

On a personal level, Rick and I just clicked. I think it was mainly because we both loved freebase. First behind bars, and later over sushi, we would talk about smoking and swap stories. In unison, our jaws would begin to grind (it's happening right now as I write this).

Later, when he fell off the wagon, I jumped off too and joined him for one turn around the track.

After he got out of jail, Rick would call or summon me at odd times. He phoned from his hospital bed after his hip replacement, and again after his stroke. At one point, we set out to do his autobiography together. The book never happened, mostly because of the greedy people who were managing each of us, and also because the contract called for me to guarantee that Rick would show up for all the interviews.

To prepare a proposal, we sat down during one long session and I debriefed him of his experience regarding his two favorite topics—sex and freebase. The shit he related was outrageous. There was this thing with an aquarium hose that still haunts me today. Much of it ended up going into my novel, *Deviant Behavior*, another character intended as a fond tribute.

And one last thing. For the record, Rick James never said "I'm Rick James, bitch."

That was an invention that first aired on the euphonious show hosted by the comedian David Chappelle. After it became a catchphrase on television, however, I can report that Rick took great pleasure in mimicking it.

Of course, as any journalist knows, there is nothing stranger than truth. During the course of our work on the proposal, Rick took a big hit, exhaled, closed his eyes for a few long moments.

Then his lids sprung open.

"I killed a bitch with an orgasm," he declared.

Like all of Rick's stories, it was worth hearing.

Mike Sager
La Jolla, CA

When Should a Man Stop Smoking Weed?

I am nosing my car into a parking space in a mini-strip mall, as directed by the text message I'd received earlier, when a car pulls up behind me, blocking my retreat.

I'd taken the specified exit off the 55 Freeway in Santa Ana, California, the second-most populous city in Orange County. Erase from your internal screen for a moment the glamorous O.C. you see on television. This part of the province is landlocked, sunbaked, graffitied and nearly 80 percent Hispanic; the annual per capita income is about $12,000. It is high noon. There is plenty of traffic but strangely nobody on foot. I've been here only once before, to check out the hook spot where football's fallen Robo Quarterback, Todd Marinovich, liked to score his black tar heroin, known in these parts as *chiva,* Spanish for goat.

The car behind me is low-slung and midnight blue. It idles with a throaty purr, an expensive toy that has seen better days and could certainly use a wash. I open the passenger door. Inside is a sandy-haired 30-something; he looks like a typical marketing guy in a white dress shirt. He thanks me for driving all this way.

I get inside. He hands me a chilled bottle of Smartwater and a blindfold.

"It isn't far," he says, pulling away.

* * *

I bought my first dime bag of marijuana at the age of 12, inside a wooden stall decorated with predictable penknife etchings in the boys' bathroom on the second floor of my Hebrew school in Baltimore.

My parents sent me to the school three times a week in order to learn my heritage, to give me a sense of place as a Jew in a post-Holocaust world. What they probably hadn't considered was the fact that their coddled suburban child would be rubbing elbows for all those hours every week with a more worldly urban variety of adolescent that lived across the city line. These were kids from a lower socioeconomic environment, you might say, who rode public buses solo and attended scary schools with black majorities—remember the middle school in the HBO series *The Wire*? These kids smoked and drank and had a lot more sex (allegedly) than the naive little county mice from Pikesville, where I was from. Some of their parents worked at night and left them alone in the house. Like Jimi Hendrix was singing around that time, they were *experienced.*

And I was there to learn.

The point is, any serious smoker will tell you that marijuana—besides making doughnuts taste better, movies seem cooler and sex more intense—opens certain doors of perception. After you've smoked the first time (or five), you start seeing yourself a little differently, and this in turn makes you see the world a little differently. Maybe it makes you a little more open to things, a gateway in a positive sense.

Over the past 45 years, in the course of my travels as a person and as a journalist, marijuana has served as a great equalizer, a safe and easy common denominator that has put me on the same sofa, log or grassy knoll as people I would never have sat down with otherwise.

I've smoked pot with gangbangers, actors, rap stars, construction workers, bankers, homeless guys and millionaires. I've smoked at 14,000 feet in the Nepalese Himalayas with a Sherpa guide; at 36,000 feet in a commercial airliner back in the days when they had smoking sections; at just below sea level on the beach of Marlon Brando's private atoll with a topless Tahitian translator; in the ruins of a factory in North Philadelphia with a bunch of 13-year-olds while watching pit bulls fight to the death—hey, all of those kids worked shifts selling crack and had juvie records a mile long.

I've smoked with a Bedouin and a couple of PLO operatives in a refugee camp in the Gaza Strip (we used a pipe made out of irrigation tubing); a captain of a 60-foot catamaran in the British Virgin Islands; a dwarf in Queensland, Australia, who was once famous for being tossed; a television beauty in her Santa Monica apartment; and a pimp in a Lincoln Continental and a hooker on a dark street corner (of course, you never smoke under the lamp).

I've smoked pot (and other things) with Gil Scott-Heron and Rick James. I once made Snoop Dogg cough with my own preferred strain, which I go to a lot of trouble to get. I smoked with Woody Harrelson in an underground parking lot using a health-conscientious vaporizer (plugged into a USB port in a hybrid car); as we were finishing, his friend David Blaine showed up and started doing card tricks. (Would you believe that Blaine, on regular outings, carries not just cards in his pockets but also a Sharpie to aid with tricks?) I've even smoked with my son—but only after he turned 18 and got his own medical marijuana card.

A number of years ago, I was doing bong hits with the comedian Roseanne after an interview at her house in Lake Arrowhead, California. At one point, after staring for some time into the roaring fire in the big fireplace, she said reflectively: "All hate is just fear. All fear is insecurity."

This statement floored me, stoned or not. It seemed to sum up all the problems of humanity, the reason for wars since the dawn of time. Ethnic groups, nations, members of the various religious flocks—it is our differing forms and contents that bedevil us. What's different is always considered bad, scary or threatening. (Unless, it suddenly becomes the thing to do.)

Sharing a bowl with someone, you take the opportunity to share a part of yourself. Some of it is physical—you're actually sitting together with this person or persons, handing something back and forth. Some of it is neurochemistry. It's called *disinhibition,* one of the effects of THC. Given this time together with someone else, engaged in a mutual pursuit, we unconsciously suspend our disbelief. Suddenly our differences don't seem as important as our communalities. If you can share your spit on a joint, the possibilities seem limitless, wouldn't you agree?

* * *

At last the low-slung, midnight blue sports car comes to a stop, and I am allowed to take off my blindfold, which probably hadn't looked too weird once I'd decided to wear my sunglasses over it.

I have no clue where we are, other than inside a run-down commercial building that seems to be under renovation. We find two guys in a room with a small vat of marijuana oil, inside one of the several secret labs in northern and southern California where a company called DankTanks.Net is working on the latest in marijuana technology.

If you're anything of a stoner, maybe you know that weed concentrates have become big lately—in the latest vernacular, you'd say a particular batch is *dank as fuck,* hence the name of the company. Sold in medical marijuana establishments, concentrates are a West Coast phenomenon that is slowly moving across the country. To some extent, you could say that concentrates are to marijuana as cocaine is to coca or as heroin is to opium; a natural plant once refined, though not nearly so powerful or addictive—and a potent medicine in many people's estimation.

To make concentrate, the trimmings from the harvest of buds (previously sold cheap) are run through machines that use butane or propane (not so healthy) or CO_2 (more organic) to distill out the active ingredients (cannabinoids and THC, the first known for their medicinal properties, the second known for getting you high). More recently, people have begun to use the buds instead; better product, better yield. DankTanks uses cuttings from three strong, popular strains familiar to medical marijuana patients in California: Sour Diesel, OG Kush and Headband. Other forms differ in texture and strength depending upon the weed source and the expertise: wax, butter, oil, shatter and crumble.

There are several ways to smoke concentrates. You can be fancy and use a glass bong, a blowtorch, a special nail and a bunch of glass accessories—it's called doing *dabs.* Or you can use different electronic-cigarette-like vaporizers designed to accommodate concentrates. The water vapor is supposed to be better for your lungs than smoke; the high (even with sativa-based products) is a little different, more of a hash high that affects your body and makes you a little sluggish, not so cerebrally intense. There are several big differences: Concentrates don't look like weed; products range in color from gold to dark brownish green. And concentrates don't smell skunky like pot. In fact, they hardly smell at all. Also, the vapor is more ephemeral than smoke—it dissipates quickly into the atmosphere. Concentrates, manufacturers like to say, are stronger and more "discreet."

We sit talking as the guys, all partners in DankTanks, melt a large, flat slice of wax, mix in grapeseed oil and vegetable glycerin and load the bullet-shaped tanks using syringes. All three men are in their early thirties. Two say they have degrees in marketing; the third says he used to own several medical marijuana stores. He has an obvious side effect of a serious medical condition, now under control. He explains how his patients, especially the older ones, especially ones who might be residents of assisted living facilities, really appreciate the DankTanks/e-cig format. One tank holds 1.6 milliliters of oil, retails in medical marijuana stores for $75 and is good for an estimated 200 hits. It also eliminates the need for grinders, lighters, ashtrays and other smoking (and cleaning) paraphernalia necessary to smoke weed. "You just screw on the tank and hit the dank," he says with a smirk.

In time it is determined, in the way things are usually determined in these situations, that I would perhaps be amenable to, and even interested in, ahem, *sampling the product.* (What the hell were you waiting for?)

An e-cig is proffered. I take a few puffs. The vapor is light and pleasant smelling, though it does tend to make me cough—the medical marijuana expert explains that the molecules of water vapor tend to expand in the lungs.

A mindful silence falls over the room. The guys catch a rhythm filling the tanks, somebody's indie rock playlist flows through portable speakers.

I watch them work. I think about how cool it is to be in my fifties and still learning new things. I guess you could say that over the course of my lifetime, marijuana has been my only hobby. Granted, I go places and meet people for a living, which is what most people do in their spare time. In my own spare time I don't play golf, collect shit or fly planes. Sports injuries have left me unable to play any more games. Writing takes a lot of hours. Factor in an enthusiastic commitment to fatherhood, and you might conclude, as I have, that I don't have much time for anything else. (Well, there is occasional dating, hill walking, and media viewing on a large-screen TV: Man cannot live by marijuana alone.)

Once opened to me, the doors of perception have led to more experiences and life lessons than I could ever have imagined back in 1968 or so, when my friends and I were giggling across the temple parking lot, bound for Amy Joy Donuts, smoking a joint on the way. What could be a more perfect journey?

A short walk leading to a good high and a huge cinnamon roll. Later in life, those are the kinds of things you remember.

I'm not sure if our puritan nation will ever legalize pot. Legislating morality has always been a slippery slope in the United States. For now, we have Colorado and Washington, and we have medical marijuana in 23 states plus Washington, D.C. And we have the eternally unfettered imagination of humankind—always finding a new way to get high. Sitting in the folding chair in the DankTanks Production Lab, watching the guys work, I imagine myself in the future: an old man in a nursing home, puffing on my high-tech electronic pipe.

A harried woman in a white uniform sticks her head into the door of my room. The health care system is a mess. She has one of those nurse-caretaker personalities; she feels like the whole crumbling shebang is resting on her ample shoulders. She uses a patronizing tone: "How are we doing today, Mr. Sager?"

I'm sitting at my computer writing something. I can tell she doesn't give one shit about how I'm doing. I look over and smirk.

"Dank as fuck," I tell her.

Dab Artists

We were somewhere around Barstow, on the edge of the desert in a driving rain, when my passenger, Samuel "Skywalker" Taylor, began to fidget with the well-traveled, anti-ballistic, Pelican-brand polypropylene case resting on the floor mat between his feet. Hazard yellow and covered with stickers, equipped with double-throw latches and a heavy-duty handle, it resembled something the modern army might carry into battle, a safe box for a delicate gun sight or high-end piece of electronics.

Skywalker is a chunky man of 32 with a burner cell phone, an exceptionally well-developed palate, and a bit of an asthmatic wheeze. A former intern for a Republican U.S. senator—his season in Washington politics left him sprinting for the exit—he has worked as a bartender, a chef, a computer programmer, and a marijuana grower. Now, he says, he's "an ambassador for a California-based lifestyle brand inspired by the culture of hash oil." As such, he buys and sells marijuana buds and trim, hash oil and edibles, T-shirts and hats. He'd tell you more, but many of his activities are illegal, even though his products are not. His and the names of many other individuals and companies in this story have been changed.

On a stormy December afternoon, we were headed to Las Vegas for the fourth annual Secret Cup Finals, the culmination of a yearlong series of regional judged events that bring together the best artisanal hash-oil makers in the country. The festivities were to be held in a rented mansion off the Strip. Skywalker had paid dearly for a room in a guesthouse by the pool. His fledgling concern, Jedi Extracts, was one of the sponsors. Besides looking forward to representing his brand, making new contacts, and sampling all the entries—some of which for sure would be "fire," meaning the best of the best—Skywalker was stoked to meet up again with his friends in the elite community that has grown up over the past half-decade around the business and craft of making hash oil, called extraction.

Cool but nerdy, deliberately unkempt, more comfortable alone or in small groups, these self-taught Heisenbergs of hash oil call themselves Wooks, after the fierce but cuddly Star Wars creatures many of them resemble. Mostly men in their 20s and 30s, they favor beards and tats, blown-glass pendants, food-stained hoodies, and flat-brimmed ball caps with collectible pins decorating the crowns. Known by their colorful handles—Big D, Brutal Bee, Task Rok, Witsofire, the Medi Brothers, Hector from SmellslikeOG—the Wooks devote their lives to producing and smoking the very finest hash oil, a form of concentrated marijuana that can be extracted from the leaves and flowers of the pot plant by a variety of chemical processes, the most common of which employs ordinary cans of highly volatile butane lighter fluid as a chemical solvent.

Hash oil (the formal name is butane hash oil, known as BHO) is a modern version of hashish. The butane gas and lab equipment replace the intensive labor of patting, sifting, and compressing marijuana flowers that go into the traditional method of creating hash. Since the 1960s, devotees have been making a sludgy form of hash oil, usually on the stove in a pot using a variety of toxic solvents including naphtha, hexane, or isopropyl alcohol. A precursor to BHO began to appear around 2000 in Los Angeles's San Fernando Valley. The first recognized iteration was called Juice. It was smoked primarily on top of a green screen—a pipe bowl full of pot or pot ash. Some preferred to chase the dragon, using a straw and a hot knife or a piece of foil and a flame.

Almost from the beginning, enthusiasts started making their own pipes. Soon the glass blowers became involved; today you can buy elaborate blown-glass pipes that cost tens of thousands. When smoked, hash oil produces a more substantial rush than marijuana flowers, but the overall high doesn't last as long. A heavy smoke session often leads to a spontaneous nap. The Wooks call this condition DTFO, Dabbed The Fuck Out. They take great sport in posting DTFO photos of one another on social media.

BHO was first widely publicized in 2009, when it won "best product" at the *High Times* Cannabis Cup in Amsterdam. The founders of the Secret Cup, Jeremy Norrie and Daniel de Sailles, were part of the team that first brought hash oil to the Amsterdam competition. According to many but not all, they helped popularize the term *dab*, which was coined to describe the approximate dosage. ("Dabbing" means smoking hash oil.)

Like pot, hash oil can be purchased legally in a dispensary or illegally from an extractor or a dealer. The categories of hash oil vividly denote the different textures of the stuff, which originates as a liquid but eventually hardens into a solid state unless otherwise prepared. There is wax, shatter (as in broken glass), budda (butter), honeycomb, live resin (sticky), crumble (like crack), and honey oil. Hash oil of a lesser grade and potency is also used for edibles, tinctures, lotions, drinks, and e-vape cartridges.

The colors range from vivid greens to golden yellows to burnt-sugar browns. A translucent golden amber is considered the connoisseur's choice. As a rule, Skywalker will not smoke anything that's not clear, even some of the Secret Cup entries. "I'm not putting that shit in my lungs," he often says, implying that he doesn't know who'd extracted it or how.

Because of the stigma against smoking, the medical marijuana statutes recently passed in New York allow only the use of hash oils, edible or vaporized. Smoking pot remains illegal. If New York is a predictor, hash oil may well be the future of the marijuana industry—a national market expected to reach $47 billion in total revenue by 2016.

Twenty-three states and the District of Columbia allow some form of legal marijuana use, medical or recreational. Twelve states explicitly allow for the use of marijuana extracts, which lack the telltale skunky smell of marijuana—the buzzword in the industry is *discreet*. However, only two states permit extraction, Colorado and Washington, where rigorous laboratory specifications must be met. "In the other ten states," says Paul Armentano of the National Organization for the Reform of Marijuana Laws, "arguably the extracts are legal when they fall from the sky."

Today, as large companies and venture capitalists rush into the rapidly expanding hash-oil arena, Skywalker and his fellow Wooks are fighting for their piece of the future. Echoing the sentiments of artisanal craftsmen in other fields, they are hoping that quality and discriminating palates win the day—or at least keep them in business as the giants grab bigger shares of the market.

For the Wooks, attending the Secret Cup is like attending a high-level trade show. (For legal reasons, the finals are considered a private party.) It's sort of a March Madness for extractors—not the only such contest in the world, but maybe the most exclusive. The regional winners were going to be present at the finals as well as some of the winners from the previous year. In all there would be 20 entrants. Bragging rights and future contracts were at stake. If Skywalker and the others want to compete in their rapidly growing field, they need to be known, to be intimate with the doings and players in their industry, to cultivate an aura of insider success.

But it won't be just work. It is, after all, Las Vegas. These Secret Cup gatherings have become somewhat dear to Skywalker. Wooks are loners. Their lives are furtive and solitary. Most reside in rural areas in states where they could easily be busted. If they are busted—as was a friend of Skywalker's who blew up a house when the butane exploded—none of the other Wooks will dare to call, fearing their friend's communications are being monitored by police. As it is, their community exists mostly on social media. Attending the Secret Cup would be some of Skywalker's best friends, the people with whom he Facebooks and Instagrams regularly. Hanging out for five days in Vegas with his fellow Wooks, eating, smoking, wreaking a little havoc on the Strip—"What's not to like?" Skywalker said in his gruff East Coast manner.

By three in the afternoon the storm was still raging, and we had two hours left to drive. The desert sky was black. Gusting winds buffeted the car. As we made our way toward Las Vegas, the red lights in front of me were a watery mirage. Skywalker was biting his pinkie fingernail, a nervous tell I'd begun to notice during our time together. At some point, I heard a deep sigh emanating from his vicinity, followed by a rattling cough. Out of the corner of my eye I noticed him reach down between his feet, throw the double latches of his Pelican case.

From the custom foam padding arranged inside, he withdrew his Mini Sundae Cup rig. Five inches tall, made of clear glass by a company called Hitman, the pipe retails for $500 and uses a small amount of water as a filter. The bowl on top, called a nail, is an after-market add-on, fabricated of the finest quartz. (Some enthusiasts prefer nails made of Grade 2 titanium, a type used in missiles.) Placing the rig in the cup holder, Skywalker reached into his backpack and removed a bottle of water, a small paper bindle of hash oil, and a butane torch.

The torch was bigger than a cigar lighter but smaller than a Bunsen burner. He pulled the trigger, a loud click like a gun dry-firing. A 4-inch cone of orange-blue flame burned briefly, illuminating the inside of my car.

"Mind if I do a dab?"

Two months earlier. October in central Phoenix.

A couple dozen white canopy tents, arranged roughly in a circle, baked in the sun like so many covered wagons on an asphalt prairie. Plumes of light smoke rose here and there, mixing in the enervated air with the smell of hot dogs from the vendors by the gate.

The Secret Cup Desert Regional was the sixth stop on the 2014 Secret Cup circuit. Like all the others except the final, it featured a weekend expo open to the public. The Secret Cup could be called a smaller, more specialized version of the huge gatherings made popular over the years by *High Times*'s Cannabis Cups. A cross between a farmer's market and a renaissance fair, the expo is a pop-up festival for connoisseurs of artisanal hash oil, edibles, and other concentrates. Available for sale alongside various marijuana products were paraphernalia, art, and clothing. In one area, glass blowers demonstrated their skills. For the price of admission—$20 per day—anyone who presented a medical marijuana license could smoke as many dabs as they were able. There were also deals to be had: A gram of top-shelf hash oil was selling for as little as $50, about half the going rate in dispensaries.

Beneath one of the white tents, in a booth rented by Jedi Extracts, Skywalker and his right-hand man, a guy called the Captain, were working the crowd with the zeal of boardwalk hucksters, pushing a drinkable hash-oil extract. Suspended in cherry syrup, it is sold in a small red pharmaceutical bottle to resemble the narcotic cough medicine known in hip-hop circles as Purple Drank, a combination of promethazine and codeine. You might call it a novelty item, but it has a pleasing taste and a copacetic effect, especially over ice in the heat. Sales were brisk.

Seated alongside Skywalker and the Captain at a folding table was an extractor named Sloth Bear, one of several with whom Skywalker works. By necessity there's a lot of collaboration in the hash-oil trade. Skywalker neither grows pot nor extracts oil, though he has done both. These days, he finds the weed. He finds the extractors. He finds the producers of hash-oil capsules or gummy bears or syrup. He finds the dispensaries to take these items off his hands. Each deal is different, but the best scenario for Skywalker is when dispensaries provide all the marijuana and Skywalker takes it to someone like Sloth Bear, who extracts the oil. Skywalker and his extractor usually take a 50 percent cut; often they consign their product back to the dispensaries for sale. Skywalker is essentially a middleman. His talent is knowing the right people and finding the right pot, making deals happen, opening territories.

Sloth Bear, who is 29, has an entry in the Desert Regional this weekend. He's well-known in Wook circles; in the past, he placed in the top four in the hash-oil division of a *High Times* Cannabis Cup. On the table in front of Sloth Bear was a large slab of fresh oil, gold tinged with green, a pungent form called live resin that's made with fresh frozen buds. Also on the table, along with the bottles of syrup and cans of soda mixer, were a couple of dab rigs and a butane torch.

Like many of the booths at the Desert Cup expo, Jedi Extracts was giving away free dabs. A double line of customers trailed ten deep into the brutal sun, waiting to taste and buy. They reflected a cross-section of who is interested in dabbing erl, Wook slang for hash oil. A father and son looking like they made a wrong turn on the way to a Lions Club picnic. A graying hippie with a pendant pipe around his neck. A withered man in an electric wheelchair. A 50-ish woman wrapped head to toe in diaphanous scarves. A pair of Suicide Girls with extensive facial piercings. A pair of high school boys trying to look like they belonged.

"Step right up," called Skywalker, pocketing the proceeds of another sale. "Who needs a free dab? Who wants a pour?"

Born in Queens, Skywalker moved to rural Pennsylvania at an early age. His father was a service manager for a car dealership, his mother worked for a logistics firm. High school in the middle of nowhere was an invitation for hijinks. "Because we were so bored, whenever some little thing popped off," Skywalker said, "we would go hard at it and just be assholes." He and his friends would drive down roads taking out mailboxes with baseball bats, hang out at the houses of people who weren't home, heckle the police, smoke as much weed as they could find.

Skywalker dropped out of tenth grade and went to work for a local newspaper, where his facility with computers and message boards became prized. After getting his GED, he paid his own way through college. From there he drifted around the country, trying various trades. Then he fell into the medical marijuana business and things just clicked. He ran a grow in the Northeast for four years; later he taught himself extraction. In 2011, seeing an opportunity to expand, he moved to California and started Jedi Extracts.

As the day wore on, the temperature continued to rise. Heat eddied off the pavement but the customers kept coming; Skywalker and the Captain kept pouring Styrofoam cups, $10 for a 1-ounce drank with soda, $35 for a 4-ounce bottle. Meanwhile Sloth Bear had brought out another slab. Under arrangement with Skywalker, he was selling (and giving away) his own stuff. Already he'd made back his expenses. Sloth Bear and Skywalker agree it's cool to travel around the country meeting up with your fellow Wooks and furthering your craft and your business. But it's quite another thing to pay for all that travel and feed yourself. Accordingly, spirits inside the booth this afternoon were high, despite the wilting temperatures.

"I wish I'd brought another case of syrup," Skywalker said, looking through the empty boxes at his feet. He would not reveal the source of the syrup or the arrangements under which he was selling it. Like any entrepreneur, however, he basically has three goals at the various Secret Cup expos and gatherings: To make his brand ever more prominent. To continue to make new friends and visit with established ones, opening up lines of commerce and goodwill. To make enough money to continue to operate.

"Gimme two more bottles," said a returning customer, a tall black man with dreads.

"That's what's *up*," enthused the Captain, taking four twenties and making change. The Captain brings to mind Turtle from Entourage. A couple of years ago, when he met Skywalker, he was working as a janitor in a fast-food restaurant. Now they're roommates.

"Mind mixing me a drank?" Sloth Bear asked, weighing out another gram of his live resin on a small electronic scale. A bead of sweat broke free from his thick hairline and slid down his temple.

"Only if you give me a dab," the Captain said.

"All you need do is ask, my good man," said Sloth Bear.

Born and raised in Southern California, Sloth Bear is the son of a contractor and a housewife. In high school, he was busted with 2 pounds of weed. Three months before his probation was to end, he rear-ended an elderly lady and was charged with DUI. He turned 24 in jail. "It was the worst birthday ever," he said.

After working in a movie theater and then in construction with his dad, Sloth Bear was hired at a hydroponics store. Over four years, Sloth Bear—who is large and furry but not slothful—worked as a manager. Meanwhile, he learned hydroponic growing from his boss, a farmer of legal crops, and from his customers, many of whom cultivated pot. Sloth Bear started growing for others and eventually discovered his aptitude for extracting. At one of the competitions, he met Skywalker and the Captain. They became fast friends and co-conspirators in criminal enterprise that somehow never feels criminal to them. It might be hard and stressful, but at the end of the day, over a number of dabs, each of them will tell you, as Sloth Bear said: "It's what I was born to do."

Now, under the white canopy tent, Skywalker grabbed one of the rigs from the folding table and pointed to a dab that Sloth Bear had just prepared for the frat boy standing in front of the folding table. "I'm ready for another dab."

"*That's* what's up," said Sloth Bear.

Everybody laughed.

Early November in the California high desert. Harvest season at Merlin's MediFarm.

According to the ten-day forecast, a storm was headed toward us. Rain on the plants at this point could wreck the buds.

All around the farm, everyone worked with a sense of urgency. A pair of men used a pulley to haul pot from the lower terraces. Inside the curing shed, three laborers hung buds on hundreds of lines to dry. On the porch of the house a woman sorted seeds. Sloth Bear was beneath a shade tent, preparing to blast his next batch.

Making hash oil is an ever-evolving art. Every extractor working today learned his or her craft largely from YouTube, chat rooms, social media, and trial and error. Some extractors choose to leave the buds on the plant longer, some want an earlier harvest. Some prefer the buds, called nugs, to be dried for up to ten days. Some deep-freeze immediately. There is no particular consensus on which method is best. Each strain produces a different result, which is the essence of artisanal erl. As with wine or cheese or beer, there is creative variance between products, a diverse palette of smells and tastes and effects.

Marijuana has two major active ingredients. Tetrahydrocannabinol (THC) causes people to feel energetically inspired. Cannabidiol (CBD) relieves pain and a number of medical conditions, from glaucoma and seizures to arthritis and anxiety. Pot is also rich in terpenes and terpinoids, aromatic hydrocarbons produced by plants to deter herbivores. Hash oil can smell like tangerine, lemon, grapey purple perfume, pine, earth, or cherry candy.

Merlin's MediFarm grows 63 different strains, among them standards like Chemdawg, Girl Scout Cookies, and Sour Diesel. Sloth Bear has a contract this year to convert about three-fourths of the farm's 200 to 400 pounds of crop into hash oil. Sloth Bear supplies the butane and the equipment; in return he receives 50 percent of the oil produced, with an option to sell it back to the grower.

Depending upon the strain and the method of growing—and the techniques, tools, and prowess of the extractor—a pound of marijuana will yield anywhere from 30 to 120 grams of oil. The oil will sell wholesale to dispensaries from $20 to $40 a gram and to buyers for between $80 and $100. (For comparison, flower marijuana sells retail from $10 to $20 a gram in dispensaries.)

BHO extractors use one of two types of equipment to make hash oil, either an open-loop or a closed-loop system. For this batch, Sloth Bear employed a SubZero Scientific brand open-loop extractor with tripod legs that he bought used for $400. It fits easily into his vehicle along with the rest of his equipment: a couple of medium-size plastic propagation trays (usually for growing seeds or clones); two Pyrex baking dishes; a supply of parchment paper; a 2-inch hose clamp; and a couple of round filters (one paper, one silk) to place at the bottom of the cylinder.

Now, under the shade tent—which allowed for plenty of ventilation—Sloth Bear introduced the nozzle of a large can of refrigerated butane into a receptacle at the top of the SubZero Scientific extractor, which at the moment contained a quarter pound of a strain called Sour Maui Dawg.

As we sat on beach chairs behind a folding table, the liquid butane passed under pressure through the bud-packed metal cylinder, dissolving the crystallized resins in the marijuana flowers, including the THC, CBD, terpenes, flavonoids, and also something called myrcene, one of the primary components of hops, which is partly responsible for the sedative effects of beer. In a few moments, a viscous stream of clear amber oil began to flow. The oil landed atop the organic parchment paper, which was folded to form its own tray within the Pyrex dish, which itself sat in a warm bath of 100-degree water in the propagation tray.

Pleased with himself, Sloth Bear gestured toward the healthy flow of golden oil. "I always wanted to make a million before I was 30," he said.

By the time this harvest was through, he said, he'd be halfway there.

December again. The Secret Cup Finals in Las Vegas.

By late Saturday afternoon a cloud of smoke, cookout grease, and man funk hung over all the rooms of the rented mansion. Beneath the thunder of the DJ's rap music could be heard the soundtrack of serious dabbing—the mini-jet-engine whoosh of butane torches, the gurgle of percolating bubbles, the continuous series of barking coughs emanating from here and there like the croaking calls of frogs in a wetland.

The venue, as advertised, was enormous. To one side of the foyer, with its winding staircase and crowning chandelier, was a grand dining room. Under a hand-painted ceiling, the chairs were filled with Wooks. Everyone had a Pelican case. The long table was littered with pipes and bindles and dead cans of 'tane. Many had brought their electric nail, a bowl wired to a heating element to maintain a constant temperature, keeping the pipe ever ready to melt the next hit. Thinking ahead, some even brought extension cords.

On the other side of the foyer was a sitting room. Like much of the house, it was decorated with faux-gold Versace furniture. A faux-gold-plated custom motorcycle occupied a velvet-covered platform in the bay window.

Skywalker was arranged on a gold fainting couch, his eyes at half-mast. The room he'd anted up for had turned out to be a tiny converted cabana. During the storm, which lasted several days, there was a nasty leak. He hadn't gotten much sleep.

Sitting opposite Skywalker in a Louis XIV knockoff was a Wook named Gerald, from Boston. The two first met at the Secret Cup's Beast Coast Regional in Providence, Rhode Island. Since then, they've collaborated on some deals. They were supposed to be sharing the full-size bed in the wet cabana; mostly they had powered through the gathering without sleep. Their rigs and torches were arranged haphazardly on a coffee table between them. Nearby, on another gold chair, was a vip guest—one of 100 people who'd paid $300 to $500 (depending upon the quality of the gift package included) to be allowed to attend the mansion between 3 and 11 p.m., smoke free samples of the entries, and rub elbows with the finalists. The vip's glass pipe was also on the table. A pricey piece, it was artfully blown to resemble a dead infant with a bloody amputated leg.

Gerald is 21. He calls his company Southie Extracts. Like many of the other Wooks, he started extracting because he liked erl but couldn't find any. Last April, at the Beast Coast Regional, he was one of the finalists. "I never really thought I'd win," he said. "I just did it for fun."

"Did you try number 17? That's the winner right there," Skywalker said with his usual confidence. "It's the Samurai Bros entry."

"How do you know it's the Samurai Bros?" Gerald challenged. The entries wouldn't be unmasked until the scores were tabulated Sunday afternoon.

"I've bought 3 or 4 grams of that shit," Skywalker said dismissively. With a lot of the West Coast guys, he's found, you can't do much arguing; they're too mellow. But guys from the East Coast like him and Gerald see arguing as sport. Sometimes he misses that. "Don't you smell that fuckin' tang?"

Gerald dipped into his judge's pack, a leather-covered jeweler's box with foam spaces for 20 small glass jars, each one numbered. As a Secret Cup finalist he was charged with tasting and grading his competitors. He selected number 17.

Twisting open the top of the jar, Gerald retrieved a small folded-up square of nonstick parchment paper, the same as Sloth Bear uses. (Having failed to make the top four at the Desert Regional, Sloth Bear was off in Hawaii with his girlfriend, following the proceedings online.)

Gerald unfolded the bindle once and then again. Between his fingers was something that appeared to be a small, thin, translucent piece of used chewing gum pressed between the sheets of the paper. Gerald pulled apart the halves with a precise movement, bringing to mind Velcro and causing a similar sound. What confronted him at last was a half-gram of shatter—think of a small piece of amber glass you might find on a beach.

Gerald brought the sample to his nose with the practiced air of an oenophile or foodie. “This smells like tangie,” he said, meaning tangerine.

“It’s grapefruity,” Skywalker corrected. “I definitely get more of a grapefruit.”

“It looks flame,” said Gerald.

“It *is* flame,” assured Skywalker, folding his arms like, *Told you so, dude.*

Gerald triggered a large butane torch and proceeded to heat the Halen Honey Hole of Skywalker’s Mini Sundae Cup rig.

As he aimed the orange-and-blue cone of fire toward the bowl, I asked if they ever worried about going to jail. After all, their passion and livelihood is illegal in all but two states, and neither lives in one.

“I do think about the legal aspects, but you can’t really worry about it,” Gerald said. Heating a nail can take up to 30 seconds, depending how much fun the user is having, or how mesmerized he gets, or how much residual oil needs to be cooked off. “I am a big believer in karma,” he said, “so I feel like if you live a good life and you’re a good person then bad things don’t happen to you.”

“Extraction is going to be legal eventually,” Skywalker said. “More sooner than later. To be involved in the community now means we’ll have that first jump in our own states when big business comes in with their millions and millions of dollars. That’s why I feel good to be at the Secret Cup. It makes you feel like you’ve made it a little bit. The people here are the major players.”

Gerald continued to heat the nail until the quartz glowed red, then removed the flame and set the torch on the table. He tested the temperature of the nail by holding it near the underside of his wrist, the place where a father might test a few drops of baby formula.

At last he applied the 4-inch titanium dabber to the inside of the heated bowl. At the end of the dabber was a glob of the entry in question. Immediately upon contact with the hot quartz, the dab liquefied, then bubbled, then vaporized. A light white smoke traveled through the chambers, spinning a tiny glass propeller. At the other end of the dabber was a cup called a carburetor cap. Gerald placed the cap over the nail to trap the smoke as he continued to inhale. When he finished the hit, Gerald put down the rig, inclined his chin, and exhaled a thick stream of smoke toward the chandelier.

He noted an immediate increase in his energy level, a cerebral sensation of floating, a tingle at the top of his head. His eyes felt recessed, his point of view at once more internalized and more externalized, everything more vivid and intense. The music washed pleasantly into his ears, into his brain, something hypnotic by Kendrick Lamar: *Bitch, don't kill my vibe. Bitch, don't kill my vibe.*

"That *is* flame," Gerald said at last, eyes wide. He looked over to Skywalker for concurrence.

Homie was DTFO.

January in Downtown Denver.

I followed Ralph Morgan, the chief executive officer of two related but independent companies, Organa Labs and O.penVAPE, through the front door of a nondescript brick industrial building. Morgan, who is 42, was dressed in Rocky Mountain casual. We'd just finished lunch at his favorite sushi place. Before he got into the pot business, he sold replacement joints, primarily knees and hips. His wife, Heidi, sold pharmaceuticals. "We were totally naïve to cannabis," he said. "We saw the push for legalization in Colorado on the news and were intrigued. As soon as we started doing our due diligence, we fell in love with the idea. I used to tell people, 'Hey, we've been selling joints and drugs for years, so we're qualified!'"

The Morgans opened Evergreen Apothecary in 2009. It is located on South Broadway, in an area called the Green Mile, an up-and-coming neighborhood with one of the highest concentrations of dispensaries in the world. The business took off.

But Morgan was unhappy with the inconsistency of his products. "We were telling patients, 'Hey, eat this brownie, but just a quarter of it—hopefully that's the same strength as the last time.'" Morgan said. "If this is medicine, shouldn't a doctor be able to prescribe a specific type and dosage? We were looking for something that could be reliable and reproducible."

The Morgans opened Organa Labs in 2010 and O.penVAPE in 2012, the latter in partnership with a chain of dispensaries. For tax reasons, the two companies are separate. O.penVAPE, which makes several different models of battery-powered portable vaporizers, or e-vapes, does not touch marijuana, so it is not subject to the higher taxes on pot-related industry. Organa does all of the extracting. Financial analysts say it is conceivable the combined companies will be worth a billion dollars in two years.

Morgan led me into a laboratory full of gleaming stainless-steel machines and tanks. Dials, hoses, knobs, and wires were everywhere. From floor to ceiling, everything looked spotless. In front of me stood three Supercritical Fluid Extraction Systems manufactured by the Waters Corporation. Equipped with a computer interface and CO_2 recycle options, capable of extracting at pressures of 5,000 psi, the machines cost about $165,000 each.

Organa makes hash oil using a process called supercritical CO_2 extraction, the same technique for decaffeinating coffee and drawing essential oils from rose petals for perfume. Supercritical CO_2 is an organic compound that exhibits properties of a gas as well as a liquid. Because of this, the CO_2 is able to flow through the chopped marijuana as a gas would, but it also acts like a solvent, as a liquid would, pulling out the desired molecules of thc and the rest. To achieve this supercritical state, great amounts of pressure are needed, one reason the machines are so expensive.

By growing its own pot, Organa can make hash-oil products with consistent standards and strengths. Its hash-oil cartridges are designed to be used with O.penVAPE's electronic vaporizers but can be used with others as well. According to the company, it is selling cartridges at a rate of one every ten seconds, more than 250,000 per month. To keep up with demand, Organa has about 90,000 square feet of indoor grow space in Colorado. It has recently bought a 300-acre ranch in Pueblo; city and banking officials are working with the company, because they believe it will bring jobs and commerce.

Among Organa Labs' most intriguing products are CannaTabs, small tablets designed to dissolve under the tongue. The tabs are sold in pill bottles, 25 mg per tab, and are available in several forms, including sativa, indica, and a hybrid. Sativa has a lot of thc, for an "up" feeling. Indica has a lot of cbd for sleep aid and pain relief. Patients can feel effects in as little as ten minutes, as opposed to 30 to 45 for edibles.

"Our target market is a lot of people who haven't tried marijuana in 20 years, and now that it's in this really convenient dosage, they're willing to try it," Morgan said, leading me through the facility. In one area sat large industrial vacuum ovens. In another, women with surgical masks and gloves used syringes to fill cartridges with hash oil.

Going through Organa's extensively inspected, medical-grade lab—where, according to law, every batch of pot gets tested for strength and is given a bar code that follows it from field to dispensary—I couldn't help but think about all the Wooks I'd met over the preceding six months. Working as fast as possible, Sloth Bear can blast 3 pounds a day with his single-loop extractor. Organa's three CO_2 extractors can blast between 60 and 100 pounds a day; the company has recently purchased an extractor that can process ten times faster. As more and more states pass their own medical or recreational marijuana laws, companies like Organa—with millions in capital at their disposal—are poised to move into the market and dominate.

Skywalker and his fellows will likely never become giant players like Morgan. But it's also hard to envision a world where creativity, enthusiasm, and refined craft are trampled into dust. We live in an age of multiple choices. We can choose processed cheese or something funky from France. Wine in a box or wine from Italy. Hash-oil tablets from Organa or shatter from Jedi Extracts. As long as there are people like Skywalker and Sloth Bear, there will be makers of erl. For these guys, hash oil is about much more than money. To them, dabs are art, dabs are lifestyle.

The last time I saw Skywalker in person, I was dropping him off at his house after the Secret Cup Finals. He was exhausted from lack of sleep but happy. He had made a new connection with a respected grower who had asked Skywalker to shepherd him through the complexities of the hash-oil market—and to split the profits.

As he gathered his stuff, I told Skywalker I was on my way to Denver because I wanted to see how a government-regulated lab operated with clean CO_2. After all the sneaking around, all the paranoia and janky connections, I was jazzed about witnessing an operation that was legal and safe.

Standing outside the car on the passenger side, Samuel "Skywalker" Taylor leaned into the open window.

"That CO_2 shit tastes like ass breath," he said.

The Rise and Fall of a Super Freak

It must have been very late, around the time that night begins to turn on an imperceptible pivot and 2 o'clock becomes 6 in the morning. The place, if hazy memories serve, was the Red Parrot in New York City. The year was 1981. Or maybe it was '82. Definitely one of those, '81 or '82, toward the end of the Disco Era, a jangled, fuzzy, grandiose time when sex partners were changed more often than bed sheets and brain cells were slaughtered by the hundreds of millions. At clubs like Studio 54 and Xenon—the Studio for the Warhol Crowd, Xenon for the Eurotrash—beautiful people with pin-hole pupils were doing the Hustle and even the wild thing on strobe-lit dance floors, snorting crystalline cocaine out of little plastic bullets, gulping Quaaludes and champagne to dull the edge. What month? What year? Who the fuck can remember? The pace hadn't slowed since 1974. If you can remember exactly, you weren't really there.

Rick James was there. His first rock and roll band had included Nick St. Nicholas, later of Steppenwolf. His second included Neil Young. He was a staff writer/producer for Motown when the Jackson parents brought their five sons through the door. Prince was once his opening act. James's trademark song, "Super Freak," sold more than 40 million copies in 1981. Later, a rapper named MC Hammer would cop the bass line of Super Freak for "U Can't Touch This." It sold millions more internationally.

By the time this night had come, Rick James was known around the world as the King of Funk, one of the biggest names in the music business. He had written and produced songs or albums for Stevie Wonder, Smokey Robinson, the Temptations, Teena Marie, Chaka Kahn, the Stone City Band, Eddie Murphy, many more. His live shows were legendary. His long braids dusted with glitter, he strode the stage in thigh-high boots and spandex, crouching to accept joints and kisses from his adoring fans.

"Between Parliament and Prince, Rick James carried the banner of black pop over that fertile territory known as funk," wrote critic David Ritz. "As the seventies melted into the eighties, Rick was bad, superbad, the baddest of the bad. His orchestrations were brilliant, his shows spectacular. He worked in the celebrated R&B instrumental tradition—percussive guitar riffs, busy bass lines, syncopated horn punches—extending from Louis Jordan, Ray Charles, Ike Turner, James Brown, Sly Stone and George Clinton… His funk was high and mighty while his attitude stayed down and dirty. His eroticism was raw. He was an early gangsta of love, outrageous, unmanageable, both benefactor and victim of his own inexhaustible energy."

So it must have been sometime in 1981, because James was at the height of his powers. He was in New York to celebrate the conclusion of a long national tour to support sales of *Street Songs*, the album that launched "Super Freak," as well as "Give It to Me Baby," "Ghetto Life," and "Fire and Desire." Sitting with him around the table at the Red Parrot—drinking Courvoisier and Perrier-Jouet, chatting up a seemingly endless stream of women—was James' usual coterie: seven or eight or nine of the boys in his Stone City Band, each one, like James himself, a black man standing over six feet tall, wearing long extension braids, leather pants, a rhinestone belt, a parachute-silk shirt and python cowboy boots. They didn't call it a crew back then, but Rick James had one; he never went anywhere without the boys in his band. They were somewhere between a family and a musical commune.

For a while, they'd all lived together in the Hearst Mansion in Beverly Hills. Then James bought a ranch in Buffalo, and they all moved in together there. They rode James's Arabian horses (his favorite black stallion was named Punk), raced his ten snowmobiles, swam in the indoor pool, meditated amidst the jade sculpture and bonsai trees in the "Oriental Room," played full court basketball or marathon games of Bid Whist, recorded in the basement studio, did drugs, lots of drugs, all the time. Rick James believed in drugs. As he'd said to the crew when he'd first assembled them: "Look at my lyrics to my songs. All of the songs are about drugs. They're about women and about drugs, and they're one and the same. That is the persona of this band."

When it started feeling a little crowded in the 28-room "ranch house," James bought the house next door, let everyone live there. He took care of his crew. If someone's momma had a medical bill, he'd give them the down payment. He never let a birthday pass without a catered party, though none bested the one he gave for the comedian Eddie Murphy, with hundreds of guests and a different kind of food in each of the themed rooms of the house.

James also let the crew drive his cars—he had more than a dozen, from Jeeps and Mercedes to an Excaliber and a vintage Rolls. Often, he'd give them upwards of $80,000 in cash to go shopping. He loved shopping. He'd stand in the middle of a store and point. Thirty pairs of cowboy boots. A half-dozen Cartier tank watches as gifts for different women. Ten exotic hides—including a lion, a bear, a zebra—for his "African Room." Intricately carved wooden furniture for his "Sausalito Room." Three hundred and sixty-five suits, one for every day of the year, even though he never wore suits, seemed to live in the same old pair of leather pants. He'd go to Bloomingdale's, in Manhattan, just to cause trouble. He'd walk through the store. A riot would ensue as women rushed for his autograph. One trip through Bloomies brought him face to face with Linda Blair, grown up considerably since her role in *The Exorcist*. Though he never talked about any of his women, other than to say how sweet or beautiful or thoughtful they were (he was known in private as a romantic), he did allude once to Linda's talents: "It's not just her head that swivels," he'd been heard to say.

Sometimes he'd get a bug up his ass and fly the whole crew to New Orleans for gumbo. He rented a yacht for a Caribbean cruise—fuel alone ran $30,000. Moonlit dinners for sixty on a terrace at a hotel in Hawaii. A $5,000 sushi dinner at Yamamotos in L.A. Along with the crew were the others, a cast of luminaries that included Dizzy Gillespie, Rod Stewart, Louis Farrakhan, Princes Elizabeth von Oxenberg, Steven Stills, David Crosby, Donny Osmond, Duane Allman, George Clinton, Sly Stone, Diana Ross, Willie Nelson, OJ and Nicole Brown Simpson, Denise Brown, Stevie Wonder, and Marvin Gaye.

And, wherever James went, there were women. They threw crotchless panties on the stage when he played. They climbed the gates and knocked on his door at three a.m. They arrived in cars sent for them. Teena Marie, Catherine Oxenberg, Catherine Bach, Grace Jones, Jan Gaye, hundreds of others: groupies, twins, mother and daughter teams, one time five women at once. All he had to do was open his bedroom door and point to someone at the party going on in his living room.

Now, at the Red Parrot in 1981, the security manager came over to James's table, told him there was someone upstairs who wanted to meet him.

"Who is it?" James asked.

"Can't tell you right here," said the manager.

"Well, whisper in my ear," said James.

"I think you'll want to meet him."

James shrugged his shoulders, Why not? He made a motion in the air with his finger like a trail driver: *Head 'em up, move 'em out*. The crew began to rise.

"Just you and one other person, if you please, Mr. James."

Rick James hovered there a moment, half out of his chair, slightly taken aback. Who, he wondered, could command more juice than the King of Funk himself? Now he was *really* curious. He gestured to his friend Taylor Alonzo, the manager of Xenon. They'd met one night at the club when the bouncers had refused to let James and his crew inside. Their friendship was solidified the day James took Alonzo along with him to buy a Rolls-Royce. James settled on a vintage silver blue Cornice. Then he asked the salesman to install wire wheels. "Rick," said Alonzo, "only a pimp would put wire wheels on that car." From that point on, James had come to rely on Alonzo to help him, as he put it, "separate the flash from the trash."

Now James and Alonzo followed the manager upstairs to the private room.

"Rick James, this is Mick Jagger."

Jagger rose unsteadily from his seat, at a table strewn with bottles of Cristal and Jack Daniel's. He was totally drunk. "Rick James!" slurred the legendary front man of the Rolling Stones. "Oh man! Super Freak! I just *had* to meet you!"

Fourteen years later, on a spring day in 1995, Rick James shuffles into a small office within the Gothic walls of Folsom State Prison, near Sacramento, Calif. He is chaperoned by a prison official, who will stay at his side for the duration of the interview. James's trademark extension braids are gone, his hair is cut short, combed forward to conceal a receding hair line. He's put on 30 pounds in jail—a combination of fatty prison food and care packages from his fiancée, Tanya Hijazi: tiny marshmallows, hot chocolate, jelly life savers (when she can't find Dots, his favorite), peanut butter and jelly, after dinner mints, ramen noodles, and cartons of cigarettes to trade.

Now 48, James is serving the final days of a sentence for assault, false imprisonment and furnishing drugs, the result of two separate crack-fueled incidents involving James, Hijazi and two other women. To prison authorities, the King of Funk is just another resident of a two-man cell, with bunk beds and a shiny metal commode with no seat: James Ambrose Johnson Jr., Inmate #J29237.

James has passed his days inside the prison with grace, humor and good behavior, prison officials say. He has worked in the prison library. He's nearly finished with his autobiography, *Memoirs of a Super Freak,* and he's written several screenplays, a lot of new music. From a computer in the library, he contributes to his personal web site, put up by some fans. He speaks every day by phone to Hijazi and their 4-year-old son, Tazman. Taz has long yellow ringlets, blue eyes, his daddy' sensual lips. He works occasionally as a model. He likes to bang on the piano and sing "Super Freak."

Rick James sits down and folds his hands demurely on the table. "I've been up and I've been down," he says, a mixture of pride and pain discernible in his large brown eyes. "I been to hell and back. What you want to know?"

* * *

Monday afternoon, Aug. 30, 1993, California superior court, Los Angeles County. The defense lawyer, Mark Werksman, continues his cross examination on the witness, a woman named Mary Sauger: "Did (Tanya Hijazi) then commence to beat you again?"

"There was more hitting, yes," said the woman on the stand, one of two alleged victims of James and Hijazi.

"Was she doing it in such a way that suggested she thought it was a sexual act?" asked Werksman, turning toward the jury. His client, Rick James, was facing three life sentences: there were things these 12 workaday citizens had to be made to understand—they were a jury, yes, but they weren't exactly his peers.

"No," answered the witness. "It seemed they were getting their kicks out of hitting someone, beating someone up."

"There had never been any sexual involvement between you and Mr. James?"

"Absolutely not."

"Between you and Tanya Hijazi?"

"Absolutely not."

Werksman paused a moment, scanned his notes. The trial was entering its second week; the prosecution was still presenting its case, leaning hard on the lurid details. Werksman was doing his best to rebut.

Werksman was a Yale graduate, a former assistant DA, in his third year of private practice. Yet even in his rarified world, he had never before had a client come to the office with his girlfriend and his personal lawyer in tow. James had sat on the leather couch for a few minutes, then asked his lawyer for $5,000 in cash so he and Hijazi could go shopping. Here was a man at liberty on $750,000 bail, facing fifteen felony counts, including supplying cocaine, assault with a deadly weapon, false imprisonment by violence, torture, aggravated mayhem and forced oral copulation. The district attorney had told Werksman: "I'm going to get him. He's evil and I'm going to send him away for life."

James, however, appeared unfazed. In his constellation of reality, this whole case was a bunch of shit, period. "Fill each other in on what's happening," he'd said over his shoulder to his lawyers, strutting out of Werksman's office in thigh-high boots.

Since that first meeting, Werksman had begun to like James quite a bit. Reviewing the facts, getting to know his client, he began to sympathize with the King of Funk—and to disdain the alleged victims in the case. In his mind, the two women were drug users and groupies, drawn by the magnet of his client's fame from the ooze of the Sunset Strip, a five-dollar cab ride up Laurel Canyon Drive to James's mountaintop aerie, formerly owned by Mickey Rooney. The place was palatial, complete with guest house, gazebo, swimming pool and prize rose bushes. James would tell Werksman that he had noticed the roses for the first time when police were carting him away in handcuffs. He'd spent the six months since he'd leased the house inside, mostly in his bedroom, sometimes in a walk-in closet, freebasing cocaine. For the past ten years, James had smoked up to $400,000 worth of the drug each year, most of which he cooked himself, though he had for a time employed an assistant he called Chef Boyardee.

Now, in court, Werksman cut his eyes to the witness, Mary Sauger, a brown-haired secretary at a small film company. She had told the jury that she'd visited James and Hijazi in a hotel room in Los Angeles to discuss working for his new label, Mamma Records. She said James and Hijazi beat her up. She also said she still had recurring headaches and constant throbbing in one eye. For her pain and suffering, she would later be awarded $2 million in civil suits filed against James and the hotel.

"Miss Sauger," Werksman began.

Suddenly, the quiet air in the courtroom was shattered by a series of thick, adenoidal snores.

All heads turned.

The King of Funk was sound asleep at the defense table, pencil still in hand, head lolling. His long extension braids, slicked into a pony tail with Let's Jam jell, were leaving stains on the back of the state-issue leather chair. He wore a red uniform coat—a rocked-out HMS Pinafore number with epaulets, stripes on the sleeves, and double rows of big gold buttons crowned with anchors.

The judge looked down at James, incredulous, the tips of his ears growing scarlet. A former LAPD police captain who'd attended law school at night, he'd served ten years as an assistant DA. This was the second time James had nodded out in his courtroom today.

"Mr. Werksman?" the judge intoned.

"Your Honor, may we have a sidebar conference please?"

* * *

James A. Johnson Jr. was born under the sign of Aquarius, the third eldest in a family of eight kids living in an all-black housing project in Buffalo, N.Y. His father was a handsome rogue with Native American blood who worked the assembly line at Chevrolet. "Mostly, he wasn't much of a dad," remembers James. "When I think of him, I think of the constant fights. He would beat my momma, and I'd sit at the top of the stairs with my brothers and sisters, crying, wishing I was grown up so I could kill him." He left the family when James was 7.

Momma was Mabel Gladden Johnson, known to her friends as Freddie. She had her first child at 13. Later she danced with Katherine Dunham's troupe, worked as a showgirl at the Cotton Club. She regaled James with stories of her days as the queen of the Rum Boogie during the Harlem Renaissance.

In time, Momma moved her family to a housing project across town, peopled mostly with Irish and Italians. James remembered cross burnings, rocks through windows. A gang of greasers claimed the turf near the corner store; they terrorized James and his siblings until the day his eldest brother Carmen came home from prison and whipped their butts. James remembers his father showing up to join the fight; it was the last time he ever saw him.

By day, Momma mopped floors. By night she ran numbers for the Italian mob, James says. Though she made a lot of money, she kept the cleaning job and the apartment in the projects as a cover, she would later explain to her son. There were rats and roaches in their apartment, but the refrigerator was well stocked, the kids had nice clothes, Momma always had a nice car. Though James would come, over time, to regard his mom as his best friend in the world, he remembers his childhood being rough, Momma beating him with a knotted electrical cord "to let out her frustrations," he told a court therapist.

James attended Catholic school for a time, was an altar boy. In public junior high, he played football and basketball, took drum and trombone lessons, marched with a hi-stepping drill team, hung on the corner with friends singing do-wop and drinking Thunderbird. Entering his teens, James joined a gang, began smoking pot, committing petty crimes. Then his closest brother, Roy, was knocked from his new bike and dragged down the street by a car. Roy was in the hospital in a body cast for a year. Momma visited every day. In the family, Roy was known as the smart one. He would later become a lawyer. James was known as the troublemaker. James felt his mom somehow blamed him for Roy's accident. Between her jobs and visiting Roy, James hardly ever saw her. He began skipping school. Sometimes, he'd steal money from her purse and take a bus to New York City, haunt the coffee houses in Greenwich Village. At 13, police in Rochester found him hiding in the bathroom of a bus and he was placed in a juvenile home for several weeks. "Momma finally came to get me," James recalls. "She asked me why I was running and what did I hope to find. I told her with tears in my eyes, I didn't know. I just wanted something more out of life. She would just look bewildered and cry. I hated to see my mother cry."

At about 14, following a gang rumble in which a boy was shot, James was sentenced to several months in juvenile detention.

It was in high school that he settled on his life's course. "I signed up for a talent show. I was center stage, alone. A spotlight on me and I started off with a bongo beat. Then I began to sing out this chant. I asked the crowd to sing along and they did. As they sang, I picked up my mallets and my tom drum and played this funky beat, adding rim shots… The crowd chanted louder and louder until the auditorium seemed to be moving. The rhythm seemed voodoo-like. I don't remember how long I played before I started dipping off the stage while the audience continued the chant. The feeling of the crowd singing, the people dancing in the aisles, calling out for more… All of it cast a magic spell on me. From that day on, music was my life."

James eventually dropped out of school. At 15, with his mother's permission, he joined the U.S. Naval Reserves. His obligation was two weekends a month. He went the first time to basic training with his stripe sewn upside down. At home, James started a group called the Duprees. They sang Motown tunes, practiced their harmonizing every day. He also had a jazz quintet; James played drums on covers of Herbie Hancock and John Coltrane, and on funky, straight-ahead bebop. The groups did well; they started to gain a local following. The big problem was that the gigs were on weekends. James failed to attend his mandatory reserve meetings.

In 1964, after numerous warnings, James was placed on active duty, ordered to report to the USS *Enterprise*. Though he made it to Rochester, where he was supposed to register, he overslept. Faced with disciplinary action, he fled to Toronto.

In the mid sixties, Toronto was home to Yorkville, a gathering spot for draft resisters, a petri dish for a nascent coffee house and rock scene similar to the one developing in New York's Greenwich Village. Many future big names were there: Richie Havens, David Clayton-Thomas, Joni Mitchell, Gordon Lightfoot, Kenny Rogers.

New in town, James was walking down the street in his Navy uniform when he was accosted by several men in sharkskin suits. A fight ensued; three hippie strangers came to James's rescue. Among the trio were Garth Hudson and Levon Helm, later of The Band. One of the guys took him to a coffeehouse; James ended up performing with the group on stage, singing "Stand By Me" and "Summertime." The leader of the group, Nick St. Nicholas, asked him to join.

As James had no civilian clothes, it was decided that the band would wear the contents of James's dirty bag—denim bellbottoms, blue workshirts and dixie cups, white sailor caps. They billed themselves as the Sailor Boys. Being AWOL, James took a new name, Ricky James Matthews, after the dead cousin of a friend. He became well known in Yorkville as Little Ricky. The Sailor Boys begot the Myna Birds, financed by a wealthy Englishman who fancied himself another Brian Epstein, the manager behind the Beatles. He dressed the group in yellow and black leather outfits, had them cut their bangs into a V. He staged publicity stunts, paying women to chase the Mynas through department stores. Soon, Neil Young joined the band. There were Canadian TV appearances, sold out concerts, groupies swooning in the front row.

Motown called: The Mynas were signed. They recorded a single written by James and Young. Then Motown discovered that James was AWOL. The record was not released; James was advised to turn himself in.

Nine months later, sitting in the Brooklyn naval brig, awaiting his court-martial, James picked up a teen magazine. There was an article on the "new California sound." Mentioned were Buffalo Springfield, featuring his old Myna partner Neil Young; and Steppenwolf, with Sailor Boy Nick St. Nicholas. "I was happy, sad and pissed, all at the same time," James recalls. "I decided I'd been in the brig long enough." He busted out.

Eventually, at the urging of his momma—who said her phones were being tapped by the FBI—James turned himself in. He received a dishonorable discharge and several more months in the brig. Following his release, he went directly to California. He hooked up with his old friends, made new ones: David Crosby, Steven Stills, Jim Morrison, Donovan, Michelle Phillips. After a few months of dropping acid, smoking pot, jamming with other bands, collecting free love, James decided to fly back to Toronto and assemble a group of his own.

Within hours of arrival, James was in a club in Yorkville when the owner told him someone wanted to see him outside.

"Welcome back to Canada, Mr. Johnson," said one of the two Toronto cops who were waiting on the sidewalk. James was charged with possession of stolen property and jailed without bond, detained by the Canadian immigration department. Nine months later, he was deported.

Back stateside, Motown took James on staff, put him up in a hotel. His first project was with Tommy Chong, a guitarist who would later become a comedian and actor. The song was an interracial love story about Chong's wife and the birth of his daughter, Rae Dawn.

Eventually, James quit Motown, unsatisfied with the glut of talent in line ahead of him. For the next several years he kicked around the U.S. and Canada. He was a pimp for a while, he says. He smuggled cocaine from Colombia and hash from India, where he also took time to learn the sitar. In 1977, he finally got the financial backing to record an album at the Record Plant in New York City. After hawking it himself, enjoying local success, he was signed once again by Motown. The single "You and I" went to No. 1 on the R&B charts. It became the anthem at Studio 54. The album, *Come Get It*, was touted in trade magazines as the year's biggest album by a black artist.

About this time, James attended two performances that would shape his public style as the King of Funk; spandex jumpsuit, superhero boots, bare chest, big bulge, long extension braids. The hair concept came from a troupe of Masai Dancers. Their coiffures were elaborate configurations, braided with extensions of horse and lion hair. For $300, James had the troupe's stylist give him a new look: long, flowing braids with beads and bangs. Then, he saw a performance by Kiss. They wore tight black costumes, had big-time pyrotechnics going on, loud drums on risers 25 feet in the air. "I knew then that my concerts would be like the Fourth of July—a big party. I knew what my image would be," James says.

With *Come Get It* hitting double platinum, James received his first royalty check, $1.8 million. He leased a mansion formerly owned by William Randolph Hearst. He set up a rehearsal studio in the great room, began assembling a permanent band.

Danny Lamelle was the arranger and director of the horn section of what came to be known as the Stone City Band. Between 1979 and 1986, he made 16 albums with James, nine of which James produced for such finds as Teena Marie, the Mary Jane Girls, and Process and the Do-rags. Making his records, James was exacting, demanding, obsessive, instructive. He had an instinct, an ear. He'd order tracks recorded again and again until every note was perfect. He brought out the best in everyone. Once, Lamelle remembers, just after a marathon recording session, James and the band were headed from L.A. to Sausalito in a Winnebago. They were drinking and smoking herb, listening to the final cut of "Give It to Me Baby," which was being sent to NY the next day for mastering. "We're laying back, listening to the song, when suddenly Rick has the driver stop the Winnebago.

'Did you hear that?' he asked us. And we're like, 'What?' He rewound the tape again and again, playing this one section. We sat on the I-5 for an hour. He cursed us out, fired us, threatened to drop us off on the side of highway." During the entire time, no one in the band had an inkling of what the problem was.

Finally, James condescended to explain: in one section of the song, for several bars, the horns, which were supposed to be stereo, played only out of one speaker. "Y'all would have mastered this, printed it, and it woulda been out there and it woulda been wrong," he told the band. "My shit gotta be perfect."

"We used to rehearse, boy," says Candi Ghant, one of the original Mary Jane Girls. "The band would rehearse from 12 to 5. Then the girls would rehearse from six till two in the morning. Whatever it took, you know, with him there were no hours. We had a choreographer we worked with five days a week. We had a vocal teacher. Rick was like a slave master. We didn't party, we didn't go wild. We weren't suppose to have boyfriends. After the shows it was interviews, pictures and we was escorted to our rooms. And they would take a bed check to make sure you were in there. He was like a boss, a husband, a mother. He was hard on us. But if he did something to hurt your feelings, in the end he always gave you a gift to say he was sorry."

In 1980, the entire entourage moved onto a seven-acre ranch near Buffalo. When they weren't working, James and the crew played equally hard. The house was equipped with a jukebox, a stereo system in almost every room, a pool table, video games. James was competitive. He'd bet hundreds of dollars on Galaxian, his favorite video game. When other groups were touring the area, basketball tournaments were held. James played power forward, was a good assist man, never a ball hog. Grandmaster Flash fielded a team against James's crew, as did Cameo and Luther Vandross's band. Eddie Murphy was also a frequent player. James's teams always won.

Though James employed a 24-hour, on-call chef (for a time it was one of his sisters; most of his family was on the payroll, including his momma), he often woke early and cooked enormous breakfasts: eggs, pancakes, bacon, grits, toast, milk. He was a consummate host. At parties, he'd go from room to room, checking to see if there was enough food, enough drink, enough toilet paper in all the bathrooms.

Frequently, James would go to New York City, driven in a van or in one of his cars at high speed by an off-duty New York State patrolman who was on his payroll. He'd pick up Taylor Alonzo, manager of Xenon, and check into the Plaza Hotel. Then the party would begin. "He charmed everyone he met," say Alonzo. "He was always on. He loved this Indian restaurant Bombay Palace. He'd do his Indian accent the whole time he was in there. Or he'd just start singing at the table. I remember once he sang Beatles' songs the whole evening."

"Rick was kind of a connoisseur," says his brother, Carmen Johnson Sims, who headed James's security staff for several years. "He liked his Japanese food, his French food. He used to amaze me. We'd be in Mr. Chow's in New York, and he could order in French. He was down with the wines too."

Back at the Plaza, James would usually have a whole floor at his disposal. Says Sims: "We had guys stationed at the elevators to give us privacy and control. We'd have suites for all the crew, and two or three suites that were loaded down with groupies—the choice ones, the weeded out ones. We called them the 'Stockpile.'" The parties would go until dawn. Often, Alonzo remembers, James would be the last one left standing. Stepping over the sleeping bodies, James would come over and wake Alonzo. They'd leave the suite, walk for hours through Central Park.

James was a regular at Studio 54, the reigning Mecca of Disco. He partied with supermodels Iman and Janice Dickerson, with whom Alonzo say he had "this *Fatal Attraction* relationship. He'd sometimes have to duck her, if you know what I mean." Peter Max, Ted Kennedy Jr., Andy Warhol, Jim Brown, Ben Vereen, Robin Williams, Jack Nicholson—James partied with everyone.

Drugs, of course, were abundant. In his own words, James "had never done a drug he didn't like." His second single, "Mary Jane," was a love song to marijuana. Cocaine, however, was his drug of choice. By now, he was snorting about an ounce a day.

"Nobody knew coke was so bad at the time," says James. "Nobody knew anything about detox. There was no Betty Ford. When you snorted it you could function just fine. We made records doing it, sitting at the console with ounce-full bags. It was just a part of life. Everybody kept a big box full of pills: Quaaludes, Valium, Halcyon. Dishes of cocaine, trash bags of weed, bottles of bourbon. It was all about, hey, good drugs, leather clothes, horses, cars and fucking women. That was the criteria for the times. When we went on tour, my accountants figured out that we were spending like $250,000 on coke for everybody. They wrote it off as payment to this employee they named Jose Coca."

In the spring of 1981, James and Lamelle went to see Sly Stone in San Francisco. Sly was freebasing—sitting in a back room at a recording studio with his butane torch and his pipe, totally out of it. "When we left, Rick turns to me and says: 'Look, we smoke herb, we snort, we drink. But we will never do this. Sly is a legend. He's in the history books. Now look at him, and he did this to himself with this drug. We can never allow this to happen to us.' And right there, on the spot, we made a bond that this would never be."

A few days later, in a hotel room in Chicago, James took his first hit of freebase, supplied by one of the leaders of the fabled Blackstone Rangers.

And a few days after that, James flew back out to the coast, went to see Sly again. This time, he joined him in the back room. They stayed in there for a solid week.

For the next ten years, with brief periods of sobriety, James would smoke up to $10,000 worth of coke a week. He had a special briefcase for his paraphernalia. It was the only thing he always carried himself.

Incredibly, he continued to make hit records. In the five years that followed "Super Freak," James recorded four albums, earned two Grammy nominations. He produced "Ebony Eyes" with Smokey Robinson and "Standing on the Top" with the Temptations. He made the rounds of the television shows—from *The Merv Griffin Show* to *The A-Team*. He was a presenter at the Grammy awards; *People* magazine named him to its best dressed list. He was also black music's most outspoken voice in the fight with infant MTV over equal time for black artists, a powderkeg of an issue at the time.

In the inner circle, however, things had changed markedly. "It wasn't a group effort anymore. We would be downstairs working and Rick would be partying in his bedroom. He would come down, listen, give his okay, or tell us to change something. Then he would disappear again," says Lamelle. "He was the classic Dr. Jekyll/Mr. Hyde. When he was smoking, he became downright abusive. Like, before, he may have been blunt, but he was never brutal. Now the words were like knives. You started taking it personal."

In time, things around the ranch began to erode, says Linda Hunt, who still works as caretaker of the place. "He got rid of the horses because he didn't ride anymore. He stopped paying for rental cars for people. The games, the trips with the whole crew, everything stopped. Fewer people worked here, fewer people lived here. He just didn't want them around. I guess it was paranoia from the drugs."

"I found myself isolating more and more," James writes in his autobiography. "If I wasn't in my room (where my housekeeper would leave food by my locked bedroom door). I was flying here and there in private planes getting high in the clouds. I was slowly but steadily losing control. I'd stay up six or even ten days straight. I had my staff put aluminum foil on all my windows so no sunlight could get in.

"I OD'd a couple of times, but it had been kept a secret. My security or a doctor I had on the payroll would bring me back.

My life on the inside was dark and lonely, while on the outside I always made it look like I was together. I felt like I was the loneliest person in the world. When I would try to explain my pain to friends, they would just laugh. 'You're Rick James,' they'd say. 'It will be all right.'

"It got to the point where I lost my desire to write music. When it was time for my eighth album, I had nothing in my head. It seemed my creativity was gone, lost in a world where smoke was all I could create and rock coke was the only music I understood."

* * *

At 4 one July morning in 1991, a young women came up the hill to James's house on Mulholland Terrace; she was one of hundreds of people who had made the trip in the four months he'd been living there. This one was a blonde with a southern accent. She called herself Courtney.

Courtney's real name was Frances Alley. Twenty-four years old, she'd recently dropped out of a drug rehab program near her home in a small town outside Atlanta. Now she was working at a massage parlor in Hollywood, living in a transient hotel on the Sunset Strip.

Alley was visiting a run-down motel on the Strip called the Seven Star when she encountered a friend of James's named Kathy Townsend. Townsend was a former backup singer who'd descended into a life of drugs. She was leaving the motel room occupied by a friend of hers, a pimp. She'd wanted to borrow some of his girls to take to James's house. James, she'd told the pimp, had been very unhappy because his mom was dying. Some girls would cheer him up, she'd said.

The girls would also serve to get Townsend some free drugs. She visited James occasionally, would smoke coke for free for days. Everybody at James's smoked for free. There was always a couple of dealers attending the 24-hour party going on in the living room. They often charged him as much as $100 above the going rate for an eightball. As a binge went on, they'd add more baking soda to the weight.

Townsend, unlike most of the hangers-on, would try to do something for James in exchange for the drugs. She'd help around the house—cleaning or cooking, running errands. Or she'd bring him a girl. James wasn't interested in Townsend that way. He called her, lovingly, "Fat Ass."

At any rate, the pimp refused Townsend's request, fearing his girls would never return. Upset, Townsend slammed the door behind her, whereupon she encountered Alley, who was knocking at that moment on the door of a room occupied by a Mexican coke dealer. This was the first time Townsend had ever seen Alley: she looked kind of pretty in the dark. Townsend asked Alley if she wanted to go to Rick James's house and do some drugs. Oddly—or maybe not so oddly, this was the second time in her two months in L.A. that someone had offered to take Alley to James's house to party. "I guess I just felt like I was destined to meet him," she would later say.

For the past five years, James had been unable to work. At first, his problems were legal. In 1987, James filed a suit against Motown, seeking $2 million and a release from his contract. Motown, meanwhile, was suing James for not fulfilling his contract. As the lawyers exchanged paper, as the civil suits wended their way through the legal system toward a court date, James moved to L.A., on call for his lawyers. He spent his time at home, sucking on his glass pipe. He called it the devil's dick.

Then, just as the suits were being settled, mostly in James's favor, he learned that his mom was dying. Her passing, he says, "was a stunning, terrible, terrible experience for me. She was my best friend, the best woman I've ever met in the world."

James became depressed. He'd smoke straight through a week or ten days at a time, women coming and going through the binge. Then he'd take a handful of Halcyon and sleep a few days. Then he'd wake up and start again. Month after month. "One of the things about it that really attracted me was the consummation of time with basing," James says. "The ritual of preparing it, the ritual of doing it, the manipulation and almost mind control that you would have over everything and everyone while you were doing it. It was complacent. It consumed your mind. There wasn't time to think about everything that was bothering me."

Arriving at James's house, Alley was admitted to James's bedroom right away. She partied with James and his girlfriend, Tanya Hijazi, for six straight days and nights. James liked Alley, he would later say, because he'd never before met a woman who could smoke as much coke as he. Finally, when Alley got tired, James had one of his staff make her up a bed in a spare room. She was given a boom box and a night table to make things homey.

After sleeping for 24 hours, Alley woke up, walked naked down the hall to James's room. She said hello, then went to the kitchen to get a soda and a candy bar. When she came back to James's room, she recounted, they smoked a little freebase. Then, according to Alley, James discovered that an eightball of cocaine—3.5 grams, about $200 worth—was missing. He accused her of stealing it, she said.

According to Alley, James became enraged. He ordered Hijazi to bind Alley to a chair with some neck ties, one from Dior, the other from Barneys. Then, Alley alleged, he smacked her across the face with a gun and poured rubbing alcohol on her waist, stomach and legs. An interrogation ensued for the next several hours, Alley alleged, during which James continued smoking cocaine. After a hit, she alleged, he'd place the hot pipe on her legs or stomach, causing small circular burns. At on point, she alleged, he ran a hot butcher knife along her leg, causing severe burns. During the interrogation, she told police, Hijazi stroked and held her hand; later, she told police, she was forced to have oral intercourse with Hijazi, after which Hijazi urinated on her, causing great irritation to her burns.

Finally, after several hours, Alley convinced James of her innocence.

"Okay, fine then" James said. He proffered his pipe. "You wanna hit?"

"Sure," said Alley.

The party resumed.

And so it was, about two days later, after coming and going several times from James's house—where she was living as a guest, telling people she was James's new girl—that Alley went to the hospital for treatment of her burns. Doctors called the police.

James and Hijazi, who was then 21, were arrested and charged with nine felony counts, including supplying cocaine, assault with a deadly weapon, aggravated mayhem, torture, false imprisonment and forcible oral copulation. Bail for James was set at $1 million; Hijazi's was $500,000. Both spent three weeks in jail. Their lawyers claimed that Alley had been burned and tortured by a pimp, that she and the police were targeting James with trumped-up allegations due to his status as a superstar.

By November 1992, James and Hijazi were out on reduced bail, living with her mom in the L.A. suburb of Agoura Hills, awaiting trial. A son, Tazman, had been born in May of that year. One weekend, Hijazi and James left the baby with her mom and went to the St. James Club and Hotel for a little break. The usual partying ensued; a young secretary with experience in the music business named Mary Sauger was invited over to discuss a job at a new label James was starting. It was to be called Momma Records.

Sauger arrived around 10:30. The trio smoked coke, drank, talked, ordered room service, made phone calls to friends on both coasts. Sometime in the early hours, Sauger would testify, Hijazi became angry and slapped her. James joined the fracas, grabbing Sauger by the throat, dragging her into the bathroom, beating her. When she passed out, she told police, Hijazi and James revived her with ice water.

The torture and beating continued, Sauger said, through a room change—other guests had complained of the noise. Hours after that, she was finally allowed to leave, taking a cab home with $5 Hijazi had given her. Two days later, Sauger went to the hospital. A doctor called the police. Hijazi and James were arrested again. Prosecutors combined the two cases and brought James to court.

* * *

'Will Mr. Johnson please rise?"

On January 7, 1994, James stood in his place behind the defense table, his lawyer at his side, waiting to learn his sentence. Hijazi sat behind him in the gallery with Tazman and her mom. She had already plead guilty to one count of assault with a deadly weapon. She was due to begin serving a two-year sentence. In her purse, she had a set of gold wedding bands. The judge had hinted that he'd possibly consent to marry the pair before they went off to jail.

Though he had faced 15 felony counts, James was fount guilty of only three: false imprisonment, assault and furnishing cocaine—all of those charges stemming from Mary Sauger's visit to the St. James Club. The jury found him not guilty on three other charges, deadlocked on all the rest. James faced a maximum of nearly nine years in prison.

However, while James was awaiting sentencing, information surfaced that an investigator from the district attorney's office may have been having a love affair with a woman in jail who'd been called as a witness against James. Further it was alleged, he was supplying the woman with heroin during the trial. The woman, who was serving time on burglary charges, had testified about a night in which James supposedly smoked a kilo of cocaine and then broke her arm. James contended he'd never met her. Hijazi, however, knew her well. They'd shared a jail cell.

Now, with an investigation of the alleged police misconduct underway, the district attorney's office was forced to cut a deal. James would be sentenced to five years and four months. With good behavior, he'd end up serving about two years. Given the development, the judge had to reduce Hijazi's sentence as well, cutting it in half from the original four years. She would end up serving a little more than one year.

"Mr. Johnson," said the judge, looking down from his bench, addressing the King of Funk by his legal name, "when this is through, I want to rub your tummy, because you are the luckiest man on earth, and I want some of that luck to rub off on me. If I'd had my way, I'd have thrown away the key."

With that, the judge banged the final gavel on People of the State of California vs. James Ambrose Johnson Jr., a.k.a. Rick James. Then he turned to the other business at hand, James's and Hijazi's nuptials.

The judge asked the lovebirds to stand. He regarded them a moment, the tips of his ears growing red. "There is no way on God's green earth that I will marry you," he said. He smiled, satisfied. Then he banged the gavel. Next case.

* * *

Back at Folsom State Prison, the corrections officer chaperoning the interview looks at his watch and coughs. The rules specify that press visits may last no more than 90 minutes. Inmate #J29237 must follow the rules. He must eat, shower, sleep, work, exercise when they tell him, where they tell him. His mail is opened and read before he gets it. Some of the items in his care packages are always missing. Phone calls must be collect; time limit: fifteen minutes. His visitors are closely screened. Hijazi, a convicted felon now, is barred from visiting. James hasn't seen her or Tazman for three years, since that last day in court. A wedding is planned upon his release.

July 1996: That is when he hopes to walk out the gates a free man. Though he has declared personal bankruptcy, there is money enough left in the coffers of his record company to ensure a comfortable launching pad for Phase 2 of his career. Things look promising, he says. *Bustin Out: The Best of Rick James*—a collection released in 1994 by Motown, has done well. His collaboration with Evan Dando on a Lemonheads song was touted by critics as the "most powerful cut" on *Come On Feel the Lemonheads*. Another collection of previously recorded songs, entitled *Wonderful* is due out from Reprise Records later this year.

Though the King of Funk remains in contact with the recording industry, his old friends seem to have abandoned him. At James's suggestion, Neil Young, David Crosby, Steven Stills, Stevie Wonder, Eddie Murphy, Smokey Robinson and Teena Marie were all contacted for this story. None chose to comment.

James looks on the bright side. The current resurgence of 70's sounds and styles, "excites me, gives me lots of hope. Gold old funk is back. People got to have it in their lives; there's too much thick shit out there. It's a relief. Reality sucks, and that's what they're selling today. There's too many rappers out there talking about death and Mac-10's and all that shit. What happened to the fun, man? What happened to the funk?"

James insists, vehemently, that he wouldn't be in jail if "I wasn't black, if I wasn't who I am, if I didn't say what I was saying, if I didn't fuck so many white girls. Torturing a girl for stealing an eightball? *Shit*. There was probably a half pound of crumbs stuck in the carpet! Gimme a fuckin break. And the DA gives that bitch heroin to testify!"

He realizes, however, that he was bound for fall. He couldn't stop himself. Someone had to. These last two years in prison haven't been so bad, really. He's been reading a lot, finishing his book, his screenplays, writing new music on his guitar. In a way, he says, prison is the best thing that could have happened.

"It stopped me from doing drugs. It gave me a good chance to get clear. It gave me a chance to rest, to get my thoughts together, to eat three meals a day, to get healthy again. I see now that I can love again, that I can love me again. I'm not a has-been and I'm not just a nobody. I'm not a cold-blooded maniacal killer and I'm not a black Marquis de Sade.

"What I am is James Johnson, also know as Rick James, who happened to let his life run amok because of a fucking pipe and a rock of cocaine."

Generation H

"Five minutes," lisps the sidewalk diva, a caramel-colored Puerto Rican boy wearing eyeliner and a hooded sweatshirt on a deep-downtown corner of Second Avenue.

"Wait over there," he says, voguing his loose wrist toward a grimy brick wall riotous with graffiti, his long, varnished fingernail glinting beneath the streetlight, indicating a line of customers waiting to be served, a dozen white kids in their twenties—nose rings and goatees, a couple of silk ties.

"A fuckin' line?" Mark asks, incredulous, annoyed, surveying the group that is queued up earnestly like ticket holders outside a midnight showing of a foreign film. Mark's eyes are big and blue. His pupils are pinholes. There is a hard kind of beauty to his face, a slight concavity like a model's or a rocker's. He sniffles, blots his nose with a knuckle. He's not sick just yet, but he feels a little clammy, a little bit ill at ease—the way he always feels when it's getting to be that time. "Gimme a break," Mark says. He's been copping Hammer brand heroin on this corner for longer than he cares to remember. "I ain't waitin' in no line."

"Then get the fok outta here!" the boy trills, launching into his best imitation of Rosie Perez, his neck unhinged, his head bobbling from side to side, his tapered finger waggling back and forth, scolding. "And don' lemme see you back here for at least two days!"

For one brief moment, Mark sees himself pummeling the little queer—a quick right cross, a smashed nose, blood all over that pretty teenage face. He may have grown up in the suburbs, he may have been cut from a fresh loaf of white bread. But he's 28 now, he's lived in New York City for six hard years. He's been robbed, evicted, disappointed, shortchanged, jailed. He's walked in on his girlfriend going down on another woman. He's pounded the sodden chest of his best friend, trying to bring him back to life. He snorts ten bags of heroin a day. He doesn't need this shit.

Mark reels away on his heavy boots, his need to cop overwhelming his need for vengeance. He heads up Second Avenue. *What's the world coming to?* he wonders, and then he frowns, thinking what a prosaic thought he's just had, what a cliché. *Christ, I sound like my father.* Mark loves his father; don't get him wrong. It's just that his father is like everyone else. They talk in clichés. They never achieve their great dreams. *Is there nothing new to say?*

Mark has been in this frame of mind lately. It probably began four months ago, when his friend OD'd, taking their band's recording contract to the grave with him. Since then, everything has felt futile and boring: his friends, the clubs, his whole life. Nothing is fulfilling. No one he knows is happy. Everyone seems to have a kind of psychic slash mark bifurcating their lives. Waitress slash sculptor. Bartender slash musician. It's like the whole world is on hold, phone cradled to ear, Muzak playing.

His girlfriend isn't helping any either. She's a secretary slash actress. She has turned into Oprah. She calls him an *abuser*, a *co-dependent*, a *victim of low self-esteem*. She wants him to join some group or to begin seeing someone. Mark tells her: He can't be classified. *I am not everyone else. I am me.* What does Oprah know? What does his girlfriend know? She became his girlfriend only because they both needed a place to live. They've been together for two years, about the duration of his habit.

Mark pulls the collar of his jacket closer to his neck. It's getting cold. If he was properly high, he wouldn't even feel the cold. He considers his options. *Think.* Seventh Street is out—the most obvious spot in town, too many East Village poseurs. Ludlow is out—home of the regulars, the near-fatally hip from Max Fish, the Pink Pony, and the Hat. Clinton and Delancey—a major thoroughfare for the bridge-and-tunnel crowd. Second and Avenue A—young execs at the southeast border of their courage.

Passing a bodega, Mark hears two men in a doorway speaking urgently in Spanish. He brightens, remembering a trip to Spanish Harlem he once made. He went with an older guy, a little field trip, call it dope-fiend anthropology. Uptown, the spots have been the same for forty years. The dope is purer, the people are nicer. There are no lines, not a white face for miles, certainly no earnest young ones with carefully sculpted facial hair. *That's it! Spanish Harlem. He can cop in Spanish Harlem!*

He steps off the curb, raises his hand to hail a taxi. Abruptly, he lowers it. *What am I thinking?* East 117th Street is a $20 cab ride away. You can get two bags for that price, if you can find them. Mark has spent almost $15,000 in the past few months, an inheritance from his grandma. Most of it wasn't on cabs.

What time is it? Only eight? How about Bowery and 3rd! Mark hangs a left on 2nd Street. The wind blows, an arctic gust. Trash skitters. Tenements and factory lofts lean in over his head. His pace quickens. He thinks about the book *Junky*. His friends call it the Bible of Dope. Mark has read it four times. In the preface, William S. Burroughs lays down something he calls the junk equation: "Junk is not, like alcohol or weed, a means to increased enjoyment of life. Junk is not a kick. It is a way of life." For a while, Mark had the quote taped to the fridge. His girlfriend ripped it down.

Mark had planned not to be in this position tonight, pockets empty, on a wild-goose chase. He was going to wake up early and see a guy at a record company, then score some dope. But he ended up sleeping until his girlfriend came home and started bitching, and by then the work whistles had blown Miller Time in glitzy offices all across Manhattan, and the young and the restless, the poseurs and the dabblers, had crawled out from behind their daily, deskbound lives and hailed cabs to the kingdom of Somnus.

Every Friday lately, it's the same. Demand outstrips supply, the count is down, the quality is down. Wait five minutes, they tell you. You wait a half hour, standing amid mountains of green plastic garbage bags, each of them with chewed wounds in the side, the entry and exit holes of foraging rats.

It's a bitch when things get cool, Mark thinks. Like, you find something on your own, and you think you're pioneering, living in some rare space. And then you pick your head up one day and it feels like you're in one of those chic clubs, in a bathroom full of mirrors—hundreds of fractured images of yourself, glaring at you from every corner, fading into tiny horizons. Mark started doing heroin six years ago. Now, to his great inconvenience, dope is de rigueur: the fuel behind the music, the route to the sunken cheeks of the waifish model, the chemical prop in films and clubs, the self-administered antidote to diminished expectations and sensory overload in an era of ennui—180 channels and nothing on, nothing new anyway, and nothing to look forward to.

What a time to be young. War, famine, pestilence, plague, all of it in your living room, some of it, possibly, in your bed. So much input, so much reference and noise, so much news and film and product. Images and ideas from every era, past and present, rerunning at the same time. No wonder everything seems like one big cliché. This simulcast of greatest hits has rendered history irrelevant. There is no vantage point from which to see the long view. There is no time to understand evolution, the way new things build upon old. It just appears that everything's been done before, that anything you do or say or think is prosaic. Prosaic. Contrivance. Derivative. Cliché. The words of choice among Mark and his friends, these children of the nineties, Generation H.

Mark sometimes feels that his whole culture, his entire milieu, is beginning to seem like that beer commercial where they bang on the TV and reality gets shuffled. Hip TriBeCa clubs like Don Hill's mix '70s clothes with '50s music, Beat antiauthoritarianism with punk nihilism, grrrls taking back the night by running their own amateur striptease show, standing off in the shadows in their kitschy lingerie, tongue-kissing boys in full drag. Punch the remote. Change the channel. This is what he sees; dazed and confused. Attention deficit disorder. Been there, done that. Why bother. Ho Hum. Fuck it. Kurt Cobain blowing his head off. River Phoenix convulsing on a sidewalk. Kristen Pfaff nodding out in a tub of lukewarm water.

Mark stops at the corner of Bowery and 2nd Street, rests his hands on his hips, catching his breath. He squints across the intersection, sees some hooded sweatshirts. *Is that them?* He bolts across four lanes of traffic, feinting around a passing car, his stride reminiscent of the high school flanker he was ten years ago. Back then, he surfed and skateboarded and played three varsity sports. He was an alcohol or weed man; drugs were a means to an increased enjoyment of life. But now he has found dope, or it has found him, cozied up and moved in gradually over the course of four casual years, until he woke up one morning two winters ago with the fever chills and diarrhea of a serious habit. Now he understands what Burroughs meant. Junk is not a lark. This is not fun. He's down on himself. Extremely down. He's begun to reevaluate. He's thinking about quitting. Thinking about getting ready to think about quitting. Turning over the possibility. It would be his second try.

Twenty feet from the northwest corner, Mark pulls up, downshifts to a cool saunter, eyeballs the action. Some people hanging around, but no dealers. Nothing happening. *Fuck!*

He squints northeast, across the intersection toward the corner of 3rd Street. *Is that them?*

He takes off at a run.

* * *

"Hey Brian, *Brian,*" Mark repeats into the telephone. "Pick up. Pick up..."

Mark rolls his eyes. *He's probably shooting,* he thinks. Mark used a syringe for a while. You consume less dope that way. And you get an orgasmic rush. But you also develop abscesses in your arms. They fester and smell. It was all too sordid. Snorting is cleaner, easier, faster. It hurts your nose, makes it burn and weep, but there's less chance of dying. It's easy to regulate your dosage, one little snort at time.

"Alright," he says glumly into the voice mail. "Gimme a call."

He tosses the phone onto the bed. Over the headboard hangs an ornate, empty frame he found in the garbage. He calls it his self-portrait. It is Saturday, eleven or so in the evening. Mark's girlfriend is out of town; he has five dime bags stashed in the cavity of his right glove. The night is ripe with potential.

If only he could think of something to do.

He picks up a pen and a pad of paper. "Bored bored bored," he writes, the beginning of a poem, maybe a song. "Bored beyond belief/Belief beyond bored/ Beyond belief/Beyond believing."

Mark works two nights a week, 4 P.M. to 4 A.M., tending bar in a trendy club. He makes $400 a night. Enough to cover the rent and the expenses. Not enough to keep him busy. Up until his friend died, it looked like his band might make it big. The group had formed during college: two English majors, an art major and Mark, econ/poli sci. They weren't great musicians, but they each felt a need to make art, to express things buried inside. They considered themselves artists whose medium was music. For one glorious year, Mark didn't work any job other than music; his band toured the U.S. and Europe. It was a shoestring kind of deal in small clubs—but hey, it was a tour. Mark felt like a winner that year. Someone who'd defied the odds.

Mark opens his Casio digital phone book, begins scrolling down through the entries. When he got the Casio, he actually sat down and read the directions. You can rig it so automatically gives the time zone for a specific city. He set it to Santa Fe, where his mom lives. His parents divorced when he was 13. She sent him the robe that is being used just now as a window shade. He hasn't seen her in a while. He picks up the phone.

"Scott. You home? Gimme a call when you get this message."

"Hey Donovan, Don. *Hey*! You there? I'm watching Oil Can Boyd on the tube. Gimme a call."

Mark sighs and rises from the bed, shuffles out into the living room. It is a third-floor walk-up near Delancey Street, within sight of the Williamsburg Bridge. Over the past hundred years, his building, his neighborhood, has been occupied in successive waves by European immigrants, gangsters and performers, Beats, hippies, punks, denizens of the rock scene and the art scene, Puerto Ricans, Dominicans. These days, the Lower East Side is a frontier of sorts, a patchwork of renewal and decay, trendiness and squalor. The newest wave is the people like Mark, artsy 20-year-olds, piled together in railroad flats with bunks in the bedrooms and bathtubs in the kitchens.

Mark looks over at his bass guitar, leaning against the wall. He walks over, picks it up, puts it down. He was supposed to have a practice tonight, new people for a new band, but nobody showed. He stands motionless for a few seconds, preoccupied. He starts toward the sofa, then stops, then starts again. He picks up his coat, reaches into the pocket for the glove with his stash.

It's gone!

He wheels around, scanning every surface in the room.

Panic rising, tiny beads of sweat pop appear at his hairline. He skates on stocking-clad feet across the ruined parquet floor toward the kitchen, looks on the table, the counter, the floor. He opens the refrigerator. He unlocks the front door, peers down the hall.

He rests his head against the cool metal door frame. *Think. Think.*

At last, he finds the glove on the bed, next to the phone, where he left it. He plops down, exhausted, relieved. He removes the rectangular bags and counts them, *Onetwothreefourfive.* He puts four of the bags back into the cavity of the glove, lays the glove back on the bed. He opens one bag, ripping the heat-sealed plastic with his teeth, spitting it onto the floor, unfolding the wax-paper packet, placing it on the nightstand. Reaches into his pocket, pulls out a short length of drinking straw, retrieves the open bag. There is a line of white powder along the bottom, about an inch and a half long, a tenth of an inch thick. Dips the straw and snorts. Once in the left nostril, once in the right.

He feels a burn in the nose, smells a scent that vaguely resembles that of a gelatin-cap vitamin from a natural-food store. His heart, his head, his limbs, fill with a magnanimous swell of well-being. His body lightens, buoyed by a sudden absence of aches and pains. An odd, tranquil alertness sets in, a sense of being cut loose from the program, of floating in a dreamy place all his own.

Fuck it, fuck it, fuck it, Mark thinks. He lights a Camel, lies back on the bed, closes his eyes. His lungs feel wide-open. He draws deep, the ember flares. His left arm rises, as if free of gravity, levitating absently in the air above the bed.

Dope is cool, removed, placid, faintly erotic. It is warm and fuzzy, itchy, a little distracted, a few steps off the pace of real time. It acts on the central nervous system, blocking receptors called opioids, which register feelings of pain. By a curious quirk of nature, the shape of the heroin molecule resembles that of the body's own natural painkillers, the endorphins. When pain is registered in the uploads—when you burn your finger, say—the brain releases endorphins to ease the hurt, to brighten your mind. Opiates work just like endorphins, though drug use delivers them in greater supply, to greater effect. Over time, you get used to the bigger kick. Endorphins alone don't really do it for you anymore. Life becomes even more depressing than before.

It takes your body time to get used to dope. The molecular fit isn't perfect. It's not very pleasant at first. You'll snort and then feel energized and buzzed, but then you get itchy, and then you don't feel very good, and then all of a sudden your head breaks out in a sweat and you vomit copiously, the entire contents of your stomach. Following that, you remain queasy into the next day. It takes at least twenty-four hours for the drug to clear the system.

Soon you don't vomit anymore. Food tastes better. Music sounds better. Your thoughts seem to be more interesting. That nagging stiff neck is gone. For six to eight hours, until you need your next fix, everything looks and feels amazing. If you are lonely or heartbroken, if your momma didn't love you, if your daddy took liberties, it doesn't seem to matter so much anymore. And sex becomes irrelevant. On dope you can't really get it up, though it feels good to be touched. If you can manage an erection, you get what they call a dope stick: hard for hours with no ability to climax.

Overall, high on dope, you have a euphoric feeling of being washed clean, of having intermittent sets of pleasant waves rolling through your arms and legs and dick and head and then washing away, away, washing away sensation, hurt, memories, leaving just a warm, hollow shell of the semi-present remains of your consciousness, lubricated on every surface with sweet numb.

Most of the heroin on the streets of New York is China White, grown in vast fields controlled by private armies in Myanmar (Burma), Thailand and Laos, an area called the Golden Triangle. China White is brought to America by the Chinese middlemen—some independent, some members of gangster triads—and in increasing amounts by Nigerians. The high level of purity has rendered needles unnecessary; it can be snorted or smoked. Seeing new opportunities, Colombian coke cartels have recently begun to diversify, planting poppies on the hillsides at home and in Peru and Bolivia. The Afghans, Pakistanis and Mexicans are also harvesting record quantities. Annual retail sales in the United States are estimated at $10 billion.

Now, in his apartment on this boring Saturday night, a bag of dope melting inside his nasal passages, Mark opens his eyes, spies his notebook computer on the desk. He has been writing a lot lately. A stream-of-consciousness novel has emerged. He is calling it *Only the Stones Remain.* He breaks out another bag, fires up the Mac.

The tracks run through a cut in a hill. It's very muddy down here, and now I can see the train. If I stay right where I'm standing now, I will be a bug on a windshield. Once I went to a pharmacy to refill a Valium prescription. I wanted to do a mellow bye-bye. The shit was out of date by two days. If you really want to die, there are too many very effective ways to do it. I guess I wasn't professional or at least serious enough about my career as a non-human.

You know, it's funny. I talk about suicide and there's a shotgun in my closet. Prozac Nation my epididymis—This is the real nation. The ones who feel, think, know too much and don't want to live in the transition to perfection. I don't feel sorry for myself. I'm just bored to death and Dewar's with what's been left of me. How bad you WANT something is not important. Do you want to be a STAR or do you HAVE to make music, paint, write, act or whatever? There is a difference. The only way you will every find success is to know this.

I hate advice.

I really hate good advice.

* * *

The guy has a ponytail top knot, the rest of his skull shaved clean—an overweight, paleface version of a ninja warrior or some shit. He approaches Mark with a buddy in tow, a suit-type in a button-down collar. "How you been?" he asks Mark, screaming over the loud music. "Haven't seen *you* in a while."

Though Ludlow Street is only a few blocks from his place, Mark hasn't been to Max Fish in some time. A few months ago, there were rumors floating around that he had died. One idiot even called his father with condolences.

But on this Monday night, everything in Max Fish seems pretty much as he left it, filled with the regulars, *Cheers* meets the *Twilight Zone*. There is a girl with a platinum crew cut and a tongue stud; a guy with an Elvis ducktail haircut, white leather jacket and matching white belt; a hippie with muttonchops, a flag sewn over the crotch of his jeans; a Japanese couple wearing huge, multicolored afro wigs.

Mark shakes hands with the ponytail guy. The preppy friend turns to the bar, orders beers for all, plus a shot of Cuervo for Mark. Mark kind of knows the ponytail guy, but he has no idea of his name. The three talk music for a while. The two friends were in a band together for a short time during college in Boston. It seems like everyone Mark meets was in a band once. Either that or they're looking to join one. In the verbal style of the day, the slumming upper crust, the conversation is peppered with the word *actually*. Actually, the preppy is contemplating a move to New York. Actually, he and ponytail are interested in getting a band going with Mark.

Actually, fuck you, Mark thinks. He feels like wringing their geeky poseur necks. He's only here because he's looking for someone, this friend of his, a connection. Waiting: another vital component of the junk equation. The conversation turns to independent record labels; who's on the bill at CBGB; the latest album reviews in the new issue of *PrettyDecorating*, an alternative lit-crit tabloid.

There's a lull in the conversation, that inevitable point when you need to excuse yourself and go get another drink. Mark's eyes dance around the room. The other guys follow his lead—they look around, too. Then the ponytail guy cuts his eyes to his friend and gets a certain expression on his face, a kind of resolve. He puffs himself up, leans close to Mark. "Hey, uh, listen," he says. "My friend wants to try some dope. You think you can help us cop? We'll buy you a bag or whatever."

Mark looks at the ponytail guy. In the back of the bar, playing pool, are several Dominicans. Everyone in the place knows they are dealers on a break. Everyone except these two assholes. Outside the bar, in the shadows up and down the street, are more dealers. And around the corner is a bodega, one of dozens in the vicinity. On the shelves are a few dusty can of food, some sundries, no milk or eggs. Its main business is drugs: Beetlejuice dope, crack, powdered coke.

"I'm cleaning out my system right now." Mark says. "I'm going skiing tomorrow—meeting my father and my sister up in Vermont."

"That's cool, man," says the ponytail guy, he laughs awkwardly. "Gotta clean out once in a while. That's what I do."

Mark checks his watch, looks around one more time for his connection. "I gotta go, OK? Try talking to that guy over there. His name is Justin."

Mark finishes the beer in one gulp. Justin owes him twenty bucks. Let him deal with these poseur assholes.

"Later," he says. He's off.

* * *

Mark is telling the truth about skiing. That's why he went to Max Fish tonight—to try and find some methadone. He's known about the trip for a month. For one month, he kept telling himself he was going to kick, that he was going to get around to kicking. And then, the next thing he knew, the month was over. He didn't even realize it. He only found out by accident. He was cleaning up the apartment for his girlfriend's return, removing all evidence of his weekend debauchery, when he chanced to flip the pages of his calendar to the right month, the right date. *Holy Fuck! The trip is tomorrow*. It was time for plan B: methadone.

A few days away from the city, some methadone to help him maintain... maybe he can get clean. It seems like a good opportunity. It's really his only choice—he doesn't have enough money right for a four days' supply of dope. If he tries to kick cold turkey, he'll be too sick to ski. Methadone will ease the symptoms.

One place to cop methadone is the clinic on 2nd Street and Avenue A. You can go early in the morning, find a junkie and buy "spit back," liquid methadone they stand in line for but don't swallow. To Mark, the image of collecting enough spit back for four days is disgusting. Luckily, in the great city of

New York, there is always another way. Mark knows a guy who gets methadone pills from a guy who gets them from a doctor in East Texas. The problem now is finding him.

Mark walks north on Ludlow, crosses Houston Street, thinking to try the Ace Bar. To be honest, Mark has never *really* wanted to quit before. Yes, he has attempted to quit, but he couldn't imagine *never* doing dope again. Now, he says, he's admitted to himself that he wants to quit. He's ready to admit he has a problem if he can't quit.

"In the big picture, I have kind of allotted myself this time to be fucked up. It's taken me six years to get fucked up. But only lately have I begun to get pissed at myself. I'm at a point where my best friend's dead, I'm out of money, I'm at a crossroads. I am 28 years old. I still have options.

"I hate to admit it, but dope is the best thing in the world. I swear to God, it's like cheating death. I'm a thrill seeker, I guess. I don't want to brag, but I've done a lot of dangerous things. I've surfed big waves in Hawaii. I like to drive fast; I like to run from the cops. I've gotten into a lot of fights in my time with people bigger than me. There must be a subconscious thing about being threatened and having my back up against the wall. Doing dope is like backing yourself up against death. It's the ultimate.

"But then there's the other side. Like when I was still shooting, I went down face-first one time in the bathroom. My girlfriend had to walk me around the living room for two hours. It was so embarrassing. She'll never, ever, have any respect for me ever again. In one way, I feel like the closest thing you can have with a person is to reduce yourself to your most vulnerable in front of them. Then they completely know you. But then, on the other hand, it kind of puts you at a disadvantage. They lord it over you. Whatever you say is flawed to them. They can trump you with your weakness.

"For the longest time, doing dope has been a great novelty, but now it's real. I've gone through the money I've allowed myself.

I've gone through the time and the people, and I've burned the bridges that I've allowed myself. Now it's getting serious. I can't afford to be a junkie anymore. This time, I'm gonna quit."

* * *

Friday night, home from his ski trip. Mark starts the old Volvo he's borrowed, pulls into the heavy traffic.

It took Mark four hours and five bars to find his methadone connection. As the guy had only eleven pills left, Mark was forced to collect spit back the next morning. Like most black-market products, the methadone came without directions.

On the drive to Vermont, he did all the dope he had, five bags. The next morning, he started the methadone. He got sick anyway. He snuck out of the condo his dad had rented, found a pay phone, called a friend who'd been in a program. The friend explained that it might take a couple of days for the methadone to kick in.

Mark did the best he could. The first two days, he was feverish and had bad diarrhea. He made a valiant effort, skiing with his dad and sis, pretending the runny nose was from the cold, having to dispose of his underwear at one point. (He'd wisely brought along an extra pair to the slopes). By the third day, Mark was so sick he couldn't ski. His dad made some comments. "What's wrong with Mark?" he'd asked. "Does he have the flu or is he not getting his medicine?" The way he said *medicine*. Mark felt like a piece of shit.

Mark took to his bedroom. The third day: that's when most junkies flee back to the streets for a bag. He lay in bed, drenched with sweat, chills rippling through his body. His stomach was cramped, his back knotted. He smashed a fist into the pillow.

Then he remembered the Valium.

He rose, staggered to his suitcase, dug around. He found two ten-milligram Diazepam (hecho en Mexico) and swallowed them without water. He lay back down. Gratefully, he slept, long and deep.

They say that the third day is the worst, and that the fourth day is a little easier. Then the fifth day slams you almost as bad as the third. By the sixth, you get hungry. They call it the chucks. You want to eat everything in sight. By the seventh or eighth, you're home. That's it. Physically, the symptoms subside. From there it's a battle with your mind. Keeping yourself from buying. In four more days, Mark would be clean.

On the morning of the fourth day, Mark woke early and packed his bag. He drove home, went directly to the divas.

Now, settling into a lane, he takes one hand off the wheel, reaches into his shirt pocket, produces a little rectangular package. He tears the plastic with his teeth, spits it out, unfolds the bag carefully, artfully, like a cardsharp working a poker chip between his fingers.

At a stoplight, he pulls out the straw, looks around, ducks his head, sniffs deeply.

His face ignites—a large toothy smile, the teeth yellow and stained. And then the smile slowly melts. His face becomes a mask of apology, of deprecation, of failure. This was his second attempt at quitting. Strike two.

He makes a right turn, a left, another right. He reaches into his shirt pocket. "I'm gonna do another bag," he says. "I'm just gonna suck 'em down without any remorse or guilt right now. I gave my best effort for the last couple of days. I really tried to quit. I got pretty close. Now I deserve a little reward." He snorts again, once on each side. He throws the baggie out the window.

"Part of the whole problem is that you can just rationalize yourself into a corner. Now that I know I can do methadone, that I can get a prescription and I can eventually get off that way, it's giving me another excuse to prolong doing dope. I don't know—I guess, deep down, I've always been afraid of finding a cure. I don't want to be without it. It's who I am."

He comes to a stoplight and brakes. First Avenue. A light rain is falling. He flips on the wipers, taps his fingers absently to the beat only he can hear. Suddenly, a notion hits. "How about a field trip to Spanish Harlem?"

He turns left, uptown, into the night.

* * *

At precisely 11:20, same as every morning, Al the Chemist turns the corner at Rivington, heads north on Essex, muttering distractedly to himself as he goes. He is a big man, six feet, 240 pounds, in an aged corduroy jacket and dirty high-top tennis shoes. Fifty years old, he has the look of a professor—long gray flyaway hair, thick glasses, a pocket protector full of stuff.

Al stops at an artist's storefront. He rings the buzzer. The door opens. "How you doin'?" says Al.

He crosses the room, settles behind a desk, fishes a white plastic box out of his pants pocket. He puts the box on the desk and opens it, revealing a built-in digital clock and several bags of dope. From his pocket protector, he withdraws a pair of surgical scissors and a Bic pen without the ink cartridge inside. He picks up one bag, turns it to vertical, snips the packet. He unfolds, checks the count in the bag, flicks it with his middle finger, notes the time. "This will hit me in exactly twelve minutes," he says. He takes a hit, one in each nostril...

Al sits a while with his eyes closed, his hands in his lap, one folded gently atop the other. Then his eyes pop open. "Heroin restores normal physiological function for me," he says. "Without heroin, I have no sex drive, I have no desire for food, I have no energy. But when I take a snort of heroin, if you had me wired up and were monitoring all vital signs, you would find that twelve minutes after administration of the drug, all functions return to normal. When I'm under the influence of heroin, I immediately feel twenty years younger. For example, when I turned the corner from Rivington onto Essex, I felt about 70 years old. Then minutes from now, I will feel about 30. Another bag, and I'd feel about 25."

He takes a deep breath and blows it out, as if he is exhaling the smoke from a cigarette. "I used to inject, but now I just snort. I stopped injecting heroin on December 18 of last year," he says. "That was the day my brother died of an OD.

"See, I came in the kitchen at 3:15 in the morning and his head was on the table. I thought he was asleep, and I tried to wake him. I managed to get his eyes open, and they flickered a little bit. Then he died in my arms.

"I have no friends and no family. When my brother died, my life essentially came to an end. Technically, my heart was beating and I seemed to be breathing, but I died on December 18, a Sunday in 1994, at 3:15 A.M. I loved my brother very much. He wasn't just my brother, my stepbrother; he was my best friend.

"You have to understand, my brother's death is the pivotal event in my life at this time. You would think that seeing my brother Robert die in my arms would stop me from using drugs. But I love drugs. I've been doing drugs for thirty years. Hard drugs: cocaine, methamphetamines, heroin. I've made my living studying and processing and synthesizing drugs. And doing drugs. I have a Ph.D. in chemistry, you know. And the thing is, since my brother died, I'm desperately lonely. See, he wasn't just my brother; he was my contact with the human race. He was my everything. I mean, you go through surgery and you have your right arm and your leg cut off and the right side of your head, you'll know the way I feel. Half of me is missing.

"Now, I have a plan. I'm going to purchase some prescription drugs, a few amphetamines, a few barbiturates, some Ritalin and some Dilaudid. And I'm going to purchase two kilos of heroin. I can get the money. There's a way I know. And I'm going to take my drugs and go into my cave and clamp the door shut. And I will advise the city, state and federal government that I'm deceased. See, a kilo would last a normal junkie fifty-four years, but my usage would be somewhat heavier. Plus, I'd like to be able to give some away. Or maybe sell some, if I needed money for food or clothes—

"Hey, let me ask you a small favor. If I may. See, I'm very lonely. My friends are all dead. You know, everyone I've ever lived with is dead. Think about it. So if you bump into anyone you think I could be friends with, I have a very broad range of interests: I'm not just a druggie, I'm interested in all American society.

"Maybe some of the dope fiends you're interviewing for this article. Maybe you could introduce me. I mean, I know a couple people in the neighborhood, but I don't really have any friends. I'm sure we'd have stuff in common. I'd appreciate it."

The Teachings of Don Carlos

The followers doused the headlights of their dusty blue Hyundai and coasted into their regular spot, a no-parking zone diagonally across the quiet intersection from the Sorcerer's low-slung compound. It was a cool Tuesday evening in early August, just past eleven. The sky was unusually clear for Los Angeles; the mystical heavens twinkled invitingly through the tinted windshield of the ten-year-old compact. Crickets sang, a dog barked, the engine ticked off heat. They sat silent for a few moments, enjoying the powdery fragrance of a night-blooming jasmine, girding themselves for another mission.

"You ready?" asked Greg Mamishian, scanning the compound for signs of activity. He was a short man, fifty years old, with close-cropped gray hair and an elfin sparkle in his eyes. A former Army helicopter mechanic with the spare, sinewy body of a vegetarian, he had lived his entire life—excepting his stint in Vietnam—within a ten-mile radius. Self-employed as an electrician, he worked, as a rule, only five hours a day, commute-time included. He lived modestly in a rustic, two-room cabin with a wood stove and no television in the pleasant wilds of Topanga Canyon, favoring quality of life over a big paycheck, self determination over the modern-day treadmill of achievement and acquisition. A talented tinkerer with a fondness for silly jokes, he was a rabid aficionado of slapstick comedies. "Mongo just pawn in chess game of life," he liked to say about himself, quoting his favorite line from *Blazing Saddles*.

"I don't know," said his wife, Gabi, sitting behind the wheel. She checked her watch, knitted her brow, a look of concern. "It's a little early. The Energy Trackers might still be inside."

Gabi was a tiny woman, five feet tall, thin and severe, with jet black shoulder-length hair parted in the middle. Born in a small town in Bavaria to a school teacher and his wife, she had come early to the conclusion that life had something infinitely more magical than her mother's middle class dreams. Since her teens she'd been on a constant search, exploring philosophy and literature and religion and politics, trying on a world view, shucking it, trying on something else. In her early twenties she was a member of a radical group that contemplated a trip to Hanoi to stop the war. Later, she joined an underground team of Christians who smuggled suitcases full of Bibles into Eastern Bloc countries. After living for a while in Spain and throughout Europe, she immigrated to America to pursue primal scream therapy. Over the next five years, she says, she cried an ocean of tears.

For both, this was a second marriage. Though they'd been together six years, they'd only recently tied the knot. Truth be told, these missions had been the catalyst. Every couple needs a hobby, a binding interest; in an odd, wonderful way, the Sorcerer had become theirs. They were, they'd discovered, one hell of a team. Greg had dubbed them the Followers. The pun, of course, was intended.

Gabi supplied the vision, the ideas, the tenacity. She read the omens, established the energetic connection, tracked the phantom, stood vigil against inorganic predators seeking to appropriate their energy. It was she who'd first brought them into the Sorcerer's world. And, it was she who'd been most hurt when they were cast out so unceremoniously from his inner circle. Greg's role was more focused on the practical. He came up with materials and strategies, added support and enthusiasm and unrelenting good humor, a valuable quality on long, monotonous stakeouts fueled with green tea and McDonald's fries. Where

Gabi seemed to be driven by deep personal feelings that she kept masked behind a cool, almost academic exterior, Greg was more emotionally detached, someone who'd come along for the ride and found himself hooked on the adventure, the giddy folly of it all. Maybe he'd never been quite as invested as Gabi; commitment was not really his strong suit—he was a get-along kind of guy who always kept one foot on either side of the line. Or maybe his vivid dreams had shown him something special, something of the Second Attention that she hadn't yet seen, couldn't even imagine. Since he'd begun practicing the ancient ways of the Sorcerer, he'd grown adept at shifting his assemblage point. He'd traveled to other worlds, flown without wings—he'd seen awesome, terrifying, beautiful, incredible things, things that changed his life. So what if the Sorcerer made fun of his sandals?

"What kind of impeccable warrior worries about time?" Greg asked in typical fatuous style, turning now to Gabi a wicked smile on his face. He raised one finger in the air, Gene Wilder as Dr. Frankenstein, stating the elemental: "Time, my dear, is irrelevant to luminous spheres like ourselves."

"I... don't... know," Gabi said hesitantly, ignoring his attempt at levity, glancing nervously across the street. She pinched her thin lips with her thumb and first two fingers. Usually, her voice carried the hard residual edge of her German accent. Tonight it sounded soft and anxious. Something was bothering her. Something just didn't feel right. One of the things that irked her most about their estrangement from the Sorcerer was the fact that it had come at a time when she was beginning to make real progress. It had happened towards the end of an evening in the rented dance studio in Santa Monica where the group practiced their Magical Passes—martial art-like movements designed to gather energy. She was listening intently to one of the Sorcerer's three-hour monologues—highly entertaining affairs, Lenny Bruce meets Fidel Castro meets Mescalito, the cricket-like being with a warty green head that embodied the spirit of peyote—when a vortex appeared behind the Sorcerer's head, a kind of liquid swirl in the air, a whirlpool, just behind him to the left. Since then, it seemed, the magic and the revelations had grown stronger and stronger. Over the months of their surveillance, like Greg, she had continued to practice the passes—they had, in fact, just come from their regular practice group, one of the hundreds of independent cells that formed across the globe. Lately, she'd begun to notice this voice inside of herself, a voice beyond the everyday chatter of the mind, a sort of anchor, a storehouse of knowledge. The Sorcerer called it the Emissary. It answered her questions, guided her choices, told her unwaveringly that this quest of theirs was supported by universal intent. It also told her, on this particular Tuesday night in the summer of 1997, to be careful. Something was different. Something was wrong. She could feel it.

"Let's go," said Greg impatiently, reaching for the door handle.

"Let's just wait a few more minutes, okay?"

The yellowish stucco compound occupied a large corner lot in the tidy neighborhood of Westwood Village, not far from the campus of UCLA. A rambling, L-shaped building with shallow peaks and a shingle roof, it had bars on the windows and a large, internal courtyard, all of it obscured from view by a 12-foot privet hedge that ran along the street sides of the property. From their parking place on the southwest corner of Pandora and Eastborne Avenues, the Followers could watch both gated entrances of the compound, each of which carried a separate address. The right side, on Eastborne, seemed to be used only by male visitors. According to the Sorcerer's teachings, the right side symbolized experiential knowledge, everything we know—the Tonal. The left side symbolized the mysterious, the unknown—the Nagual. The Sorcerer was also known as the Nagual, the last of a line of shamans that stretched back thousands of years to the Toltecs, the pre-Hispanic Indians who inhabited the central and northern regions of Mexico prior to the Mayans. The left entrance, on Pandora, was used by the Sorcerer and his women: the three

Witches, the Chacmols, the Blue Scout, the Electric Warrior, the other female members of the inner circle. The Followers called it Pandora's gate.

To the rest of the world, the Sorcerer was known as Carlos Castaneda. In 1968, at the height of the psychedelic age, he had published *The Teachings of Don Juan: A Yaqui Way of Knowledge*, the first of twelve books describing his apprenticeship in the deserts of Mexico to an Indian shaman, and his journeys to the "separate reality" of the sorcerers' worlds. Like Herman Hesse's *Steppenwolf* and Aldous Huxley's *The Doors of Perception*, *The Teachings of Don Juan* and its sequels became essential reading for legions of truth seekers over the next three decades. Castaneda himself became a cult figure—seldom seen, nearly mythological, a cross between Timothy Leary and L. Ron Hubbard: a short, dapper, nut-brown Buddha-with-an-attitude who likened his own appearance to a Mexican bellhop.

Though the Sorcerer had ten million books in print in seventeen languages, he had lived in wily anonymity for nearly 30 years, doing his best, in his own words, to become "as inaccessible as possible." Most people surmised that he had a house somewhere in the Sonoran desert, where he'd studied with his own teacher, a leathery old Indian *brujo* named Don Juan Matus, who'd taken his body and his boots and disembarked in a flash of light for the Second Attention many years ago, leaving Castaneda behind to close out his line "with a golden clasp." In truth, Castaneda had lived and written most of that time right here in Westwood Village, a neighborhood of students and professors nor far from Beverly Hills. In truth, there were many things that people surmised about the Sorcerer that weren't remotely factual. The Followers, over the course of their investigations, had begun to figure it out. They were particularly proud of their videos. A major tenet of the Sorcerer's way was erasing personal history; he never allowed himself to be photographed or tape recorded. The last major legitimate interview he'd given was to *Time* in 1972; even they couldn't persuade him to pose for a full-face picture. The magazine ended up running an abstract drawing on the cover. The story described Castaneda as "an enigma wrapped in a mystery wrapped in a tortilla."

For more than eighteen months now, at least three times a week, Greg and Gabi had made these clandestine pilgrimages. They followed the Sorcerer and his party to restaurants and movies, to inner-circle practice groups. They video-taped him at every opportunity; they'd collected hours of raw footage, the only such cache of its kind.

The Followers weren't sure, exactly, what they were after, but they were certainly not on the trail. On the one hand, what they were doing felt kind of tacky and intrusive, like they were peeping toms or paparazzi, or maybe more like they were children watching their parents have sex. On the other, it felt like a legitimate—albeit amateur—anthropological exercise. The Sorcerer himself had earned a Ph.D. in anthropology from UCLA; his third book, *Journey to Ixlam*, had served as his thesis. His own journey had begun as a undergraduate inquiry into ethnobotany, a study of the natural hallucinogenic plants of the southwest. In a way, the Followers considered their actions a sort of academic homage. And besides, they knew in their hearts that their motives were pure, that their energetic connection was strong and true. They meant no harm to the Sorcerer. Indeed, they liked him. They respected him. They just wanted to be close. The Sorcerer always talked about seeking non-ordinary reality. It was hard to explain, but this was theirs.

At last, Greg and Gabi exited the Hyundai. They clicked the doors quietly closed, crossed the street, stepping carefully, wearing dark clothes. As was their custom, they started at the Eastborne side of the property, began working their way nonchalantly along the perimeter, arm in arm, like a couple on their evening constitutional. They'd taken a few steps when suddenly, out of the hedge in from of them, there emerged a family of raccoons—two adults, two babies, in a single-file line. Raccoons were certainly not uncommon in the area, but the Followers had been to the neighborhood at all times of day and night and had never noticed any before. They watched raptly as the furry critters perambulated unhurriedly west-bound along the sidewalk, a darling little Disney grouping. The last one in line was a bit plump. It struggled to keep up.

The Followers followed the raccoons around the corner, north on Pandora. Twice, the mother broke rank, circled around, coaxed the fat baby with her nose to hurry up, then went back to her place in line. When they reached the gate used by the Sorcerer, the Witches and the rest—Pandora's Gate—the raccoons turned abruptly right and filed through the hedge. The father, the mother, the first baby disappeared. The last one, the fat one, stopped and turned around. He looked at Greg and Gabi for a long moment, a beckoning type of expression, dark eyes sparkling from within his dark mask, as if to say: "Follow me."

Greg took a step forward. The fat baby vanished through the hedge. Greg took another step forward, bent down to see where he'd gone. A large black moth flew out of the hedge. It hovered in the air for a second or two, right in front of his face, so close that he could feel the disturbance of the air, the flutter of tiny wings tickling the tip of his ample Armenian nose. A palpable sense of alarm overcame him, a strong suggestion to Keep Out. He stood up quickly, his eyes like saucers. "Whoa!" he exclaimed, a stage whisper. "Did you see that?"

Gabi just looked at him. She couldn't even speak.

For several long moments the Followers stood riveted to their places on the sidewalk. They felt a weird tingling up and down their spines. The hair on the back of Greg's neck stood on end. Crickets sang, a dog barked, the leaves on a nearby fig tree rustled in the breeze. And then … and then....

Nothing.

Greg looked at Gabi. Gabi looked at Greg. He raised his hands, palms up, shrugged his shoulders. Then he nodded his head toward the Sorcerer's driveway, twenty feet away to the north. Gabi cut her eyes toward the driveway, then back to

Greg. She knitted her brow, a look of concern, then took his arm. Slowly, they strolled toward the driveway, toward the large trash can at the curb. Greg reached over, opened the top of the can, peered inside.

Greg looked north, then south. Then, grinning triumphantly, like an archeologist unearthing a pre-Cambrian pot, he began removing bags, translucent white plastic numbers secured at the top with twist-ties. He handed three bags to Gabi, took the remaining four himself.

Neither Gabi nor Greg quite remembered which one of them first came up with the idea of taking the Sorcerer's trash. It just sort of happened spontaneously one night. By chance they'd come on a Tuesday; cans were at curbs all over the neighborhood for trash collection the next day. As the night dragged on, the Followers watched as a cast of marginal characters came one by one on foot into the neighborhood to dig for recyclables. If the homeless could rifle the Sorcerer's trash, they figured, why couldn't they?

Andy so it was that Tuesday nights became Trash Night. Every week, late in the evening, after practicing their Magical Passes with a group of like-minded (though less literal) followers at a rented dance studio in Santa Monica, Greg and Gabi would drive the short distance to the Sorcerer's compound and liberate his trash. Once home in their cabin in Topanga Canyon, they'd light a fire in the wood stove, sit on the floor before it, and begin studying the contents of the bags, one of them at a time, slowly putting together a puzzle picture of the life of the great and mysterious man. Whatever looked important or significant they kept. Of the leavings, whatever burned went up in smoke.

As you would guess, the Followers learned a great many things from the Sorcerer's trash. They learned that the septuagenarian Sorcerer, who was said to live in celibate solitude, co-habituated with at least five women—two of the three Witches (powerful practitioners and best-selling authors themselves, who claimed that they had also studied Don Juan), a fiftyish caretaker, a young woman he'd adopted and a disabled old woman who was said to have been "energetically damaged" many years ago during her studies with Don Juan. The Sorcerer and the Witches, who were in their sixties, ate a lot of chicken and eggs—the mounds of bones and shells rankled the Follower's vegetarian sensibilities, stunk up their tiny cabin. They had a fondness for ceramic snakes and Mexican earthenware. Someone in the compound was clumsy: things were frequently broken and discarded; they didn't seem to care for making repairs. The women had a taste for fine clothes—Armani, Barneys, Neiman Marcus. They didn't believe in thrift stores. When they were finished with an item of apparel they would cut it to pieces and throw it away. Sometimes they were not so thorough—Gabi often wore a pair of DKNY leggings they had forgotten to cut up. Later she would find a leather jacket that belonged to one of the Witches. A corduroy jacket with leather elbow patches had belonged to the Sorcerer himself. It fit Greg perfectly; he wore it everywhere, even to practice group. It was his fondest possession.

The Sorcerer and the Witches, the Followers discovered, used wooden stick matches to clear the smells in their bathrooms. They loved word games, anagrams and crossword puzzles. They cut their own hair. There was mail addressed to dozens of different people—over time, the Followers figured out that each of the occupants of the compound had several different aliases. They subscribed to *The Nation* and to *The New Republic*. They loved German chocolates and Diet Pepsi, little airline bottles of vodka, Kotex Light Days pads. There were insulin syringes and acupuncture needles, Chinese paper lanterns, red-handled garden clippers, a prescription for phenobarbital, assorted baby blue boxes from Tiffany's, literature on health foods and liver cancer, check stubs and bank statements and legal papers, copies of royalty checks, brochures for luxury yachts, ticket stubs from a trip to Hawaii, communications from fans and psychos, tapes full of answering machine messages, a list of home phone numbers for the entire inner circle, Someone in the compound was fond of Eco-tours and Julio Iglesias. The Sorcerer himself seemed overly fond of Las Vegas weddings. Found in the trash were certificates indicating that the Sorcerer had legally married two of the Witches, in ceremonies dated two days apart in September of 1993. A records check confirms the marriages, along with several others between the Witches and male members of the inner circle, including the Sorcerer's literary agent, and the author Bruce Wagner, who gave a lengthy and obtuse interview for this story about his association with the Sorcerer but refused to divulge specific details.

Now, on this cool Tuesday night in August, loaded down with their latest gleanings, seven white plastic bags of trash, the Followers walked south on Pandora, heading for their car. As they passed the gate, Gabi noticed, in the far corner of her peripheral vision, a white-clad form leaving the house. She stepped up her pace, but it was too late.

"Hey!"

The Followers froze, turned around. Out of the gate came one of the Chacmols, a thirtyish woman with close cropped hair. The Followers had come to know her during their time with the inner circle, The Chacmols were named for the massive statues of the "fierce dreamer guardians" that stood watch at the Mayan pyramids of Tula and Yucatan in Mexico. On a daily basis, the Sorcerer's Chacmols were bodyguards and helpers. At practice sessions and at paid seminars, they demonstrated the Magical Passes, aerobic movements with names like The Saber Tooth Tiger Breath, The Being From the Ground, and The Crustacean Long Form.

The Chacmol looked at Greg and Gabi with flames in her eyes. "What do you think you're doing?' she thundered.

"It's only *trash*," said Gabi. Oddly, she didn't feel nervous at all, In fact, she felt preternaturally calm, as if someone had disconnected the wires to her fight/flight response. Even her perspective had shifted. It was like she wasn't present at all, like she was watching the whole scene in third person.

The fierce Chacmol ripped the trash bags from Gabi's hands, gestured for Greg to put his down. "You'll never get close to us again," she hissed, gathering up the bags.

That's what you think, thought Greg. He, too, felt inordinately calm. He crooked his arm and Gabi took it, and they turned nonchalantly in the direction of their car.

Walking away, Greg called cheerily over his shoulder, "Tell Carlos we said hello."

* * *

There was a knock at the door, and Margaret Runyan smiled quizzically at her gentleman caller, a handsome Jordanian businessman she'd been seeing almost daily for the past two weeks. "Now who could *that* be at this hour?" she sang coquettishly, setting down her cup and saucer, patting his knee, rising from the chintz-covered sofa. Though she'd lived in Los Angeles for nearly fifteen years, her voice still carried the demure, lilting cadence of Charleston, West Virginia. She'd grown up on a dairy farm, the eldest of six children, her daddy's favorite, a sickly little bookworm with jet black hair, Coke-bottle glasses and startling, gold-flecked blue eyes.

It was January 1960, Margaret had just returned from dinner with her wealthy suitor at a fancy Middle Eastern restaurant, They'd sat on the floor on pillows, eating with their fingers, watching the belly dancers, drinking copious amounts of red wine. She was resplendent, as always, on this mid-January evening in 1960, dressed in a clingy black knit cocktail dress with a scoop neckline by the popular designer Claire McCardle. A cousin of the writer Damon Runyon, Margaret was 39 years old, with porcelain skin and Cleopatra bangs, a short strand of pearls around her neck. Though she considered herself unattractive—owing mostly, one would guess, to the thick framed glasses she wore—Margaret was tall and lithe with an ample bosom. Men were all the time telling her, in the parlance of the day, that she was "really put together." She lived rent-free in an apartment building owned by her aunt, a dress designer. Margaret herself had been bitten at an early age by the fashion bug: she spent much of her paycheck on clothes, many of which were handmade by a South American seamstress. Years earlier, she'd come close to marrying pulp-novelist Louis L'Amour. He penned beautiful love poems to her but lacked an automobile; they went everywhere by bus—she wrote him off prematurely as a failure. As it was, Margaret had been engaged several times to rather eccentric men, and had been married twice, first to a poet and then to a mafia-connected real estate tycoon. Both men insisted she quit her job as chief operator at Pacific Bell and become a full-time housewife. Neither union lasted more than six months.

An odd combination of career gal and man's woman, Margaret was an early prototype of a postmodern Feminist, who believed in paying her own way and. making her own decisions, living a life unbeholden to anyone. The great failure of her life, she would later come to figure, was thinking she had to marry a man in order to sleep with him. She was also an early prototype of another postmodern character, the New Age Seeker. Margaret had a keen interest in what were known at the time as the pseudo-sciences—numerology, astrology, parapsychology—and was well-read in philosophy and religion and literature. Herman Hesse and Aldous Huxley were among her favorite writers. Her favorite historical figure was The Buddha. She was also an avid student of a popular mystic from Barbados named Neville Goddard. A spellbinding lecturer with legions of followers, Neville believed that a person could alter the future and achieve personal goals through the manipulation of their dreams, something he called "controlled imagination." Goddard's self-avowed personal goal—promoted through paid seminars, a weekly television show and a popular self-published book called *The Search*—was to shake his disciples out of the dangerous ruts of their ordinary, real world perceptions: to help them, in his words, "To Go Beyond." Goddard believed in erasing personal history, awakening the untapped portions of the imagination, cutting ties with friends and loved ones. He preached something he called the *I AM*, an invocation of the God-like within all of us. Goddard was also said to be imbued with special powers. Sometimes, when he lectured, his face appeared to glow. On several occasions, he was spotted simultaneously in two different places; he claimed to have the ability to generate an "energetic double."

Margaret clicked across the hardwood floor in her sexy black pumps, peered through the peep hole in the door of her fifth floor apartment. Standing in the hallway in the dark olive suit she'd bought him was the short, nut brown, South American anthropology student she'd been dating for the last five years. He called himself Carlos Arana; he was enrolled at UCLA as Carlos Castaneda. They'd had a falling out just before Christmas. She hadn't seen him since. From the appearance of the cozy scene inside her apartment, she hadn't been crushed by his absence. She opened the door about eight inches, stuck out her face. Her blue eyes, framed by her bangs, magnified by her glasses, appeared enormous, "Carlos!" she exclaimed, somewhat abashedly. "You didn't tell me you were coming."

"I'd like to meet your friend," Carlos said calmly in his accented English. He was a slim man, five foot five, with the broad nose, high cheekbones, ample chest and short legs of a high-country Indian, A curly lock of brillianteened black hair hung down roguishly over his forehead, His eyes were large and brown; the left iris floated out a bit, giving the impression that one eye was always looking at something beyond. Though not handsome in a classical sense, Margaret found Carlos to be wildly charming, incredibly magnetic. He called her Margarita or Mayaya; it sounded so exotic when he whispered into her ear. Sometimes, he would listen intently while she spoke, riveting her with his deep eyes, drinking in her soul. At other times, it was if he was alone on a stage, in a spotlight only he could see, riffing brilliantly, passionately, manically for hours at a time, speaking of his life, his art, his dreams and fears and desires. Though he was shy around people he didn't know, he came alive in more intimate settings. He had a gift for storytelling and an earthy sense of humor, and he was so present, so absolutely directed, that social intercourse with him was a palpable, exhausting experience—like being drenched by successive sets of huge waves of pure energy, energy directed only at her.

Somehow, over the five years of their association, in his very odd, very intense way, Carlos had made Margaret feel like she was the only woman on earth, the only person in the whole world who mattered, who could possibly understand—except for those frequent periods when he would disappear, often for weeks at time. It was the tradeoff of being with Carlos, she had come to learn. In certain respects, it made her feel terrible: Margaret really and truly loved Carlos, more than anyone before. He didn't have to give her anything or do anything for her, she was just happy to be with him. When he was gone, she felt as if something very important was missing. In other respects, however, his erratic attentions suited her just fine. She'd always had a problem with commitment. If he could be independent, then so could she.

"I don't want you to come in," said Margaret, speaking through the partially opened door. "Please go away. We'll talk later."

"No," Carlos said. "I just want to come in and say hello, speak with him a few minutes."

As usual, Margaret's will was no match for Carlos's. Since the first time she'd laid eyes on him—a brief, chance meeting at her dressmakers' house—she'd been deeply smitten. The second time she saw him—she'd called the dressmaker and insisted on another fitting, hoping the dark stranger would be there again—they'd spoken for a bit. He told her he was a painter, a writer, a sculptor. He said he'd love the opportunity to show her his paintings, to do a bust of her in terra cotta, his specialty. At an opportune moment, when the dressmaker's pretty daughter was out of the room, Margaret slipped him a copy of Goddard's book, *The Search*, inscribed with her name and address, which she'd just happened to bring along to the fitting.

From that night on, Margaret practiced Goddard's techniques of "controlled imagination," hoping to summon Carlos to her side. Every evening, before she fell asleep, she'd lie in bed and concentrate on her personal goal. Goddard taught that the sleeping state sealed instructions given to the unconscious mind, that dreams could become reality if properly nurtured. Six months later, at nine p.m. one Friday evening in June 1956, her goal was finally realized. The doorbell rang and Carlos walked into her life, picking right up where they'd left off acting as if they'd met only yesterday. Their involvement would span the next decade and a half.

Ten years younger than Margaret, Carlos was a sophomore at Los Angeles Community College, majoring in psychology. He told her he'd been born in Italy on Christmas Day, 1931, the product of an illicit union between a 16-year-old student at a Swiss finishing school and a visiting Brazilian professor. Shortly after his birth, he said, he was taken by his maternal aunt back to São Paulo to be raised. At 15, after being expelled from a prestigious private school, he'd begun traveling the world, studying art in Italy, Montreal and New York before coming to Los Angeles to continue his education. He also said he was a veteran of U.S. Army Intelligence. He was vague about his service, mentioning both Korea and Spain; a long ugly scar that stretched from his abdomen to his groin was the result of a bayonet wound, he said.

Carlos and Mayaya seemed a perfect match—two passionate, keen, eccentric minds who'd been lucky enough to cross paths. Though Carlos had very little money—to support his studies, he worked variously as a cab driver, grocery stock clerk, a liquor delivery man, an artist for Mattel toys, an accountant in a tony dress shop—Margaret was comfortable and generous. They attended concerts and plays, lectures and readings and art openings. They frequented the beatnik coffee houses that had begun to spring up along Hollywood Boulevard, rubbing shoulders with Alan Ginsberg and Jack Kerouac. Gradually, Carlos's interest in painting and sculpture began to fade; he took to carrying a three ring binder with him everywhere, filling it with romantic poetry and prose. One of his poems won a contest and was printed in the LACC student newspaper.

Carlos had a particular fondness for movies: Ingmar Bergman classics, B-grade horror pictures, Russian films. He was fascinated by all things Russian, particularly Soviet Premier Nikita Khrushchev, who had recently taken power in Moscow. In Carlos's eyes, Khrushchev was a determined leader who had come up from the bottom rung of society to grab the reins of one of the most powerful countries in the world. Over time, Carlos developed the fantasy that Margaret would one day meet the great man. To this end, he encouraged her to take her college entrance exams, then helped her enroll in a night-school Russian language course, which she continued for several years.

A dapper man who favored fedoras and pastel Don Loper shirts, nicely pressed slacks and highly polished shoes, Carlos cut his own hair, tailored his own clothes. He'd add months of wear to a shirt by removing a frayed collar, turning it inside out and then sewing it back on, a skill he learned either in the Army or while living with a band of gypsies in Italy—that story, like many, frequently changed. He was partial to Mexican food, Chinese Dim Sum and pizza, long walks on the beach, nightclubs, fine department stores. In a university community populated overwhelmingly with Caucasians, he seemed insecure about his height, his thick accent, his dark skin. On occasion, for reasons Margaret could never fathom, he told people he was a Hasidic Jew. Another thing she could never fathom is why they never had intercourse together. Though Carlos avidly enjoyed giving her pleasure orally, it went no further than that.

Having been exposed by Margaret to her favorite writers—Huxley, Hesse, Goddard and the behaviorist J. R. Rhine—Carlos became an avid participant in bull-sessions with their like-minded friends, holding forth on subjects ranging from astral projection to trance running to ESP. The cozy spirited gatherings, usually held at the apartment of a friend, would run into the wee hours, fueled by Carlos's favorite wine, Mateus Rose, which he jokingly referred to as "my most valuable teacher." His favorite subject, by far, was Huxley's experiments with mescaline and alternate realities; he chose the topic for a term paper for his second year English class at LACC.

After he received his associate's degree, Carlos enrolled in the anthropology department at UCLA, a change of direction influenced by the publication of a book called *The Sacred Mushroom*, by Andrija Puharich. The book dealt with Puharich's work with a Dutch sculptor who could recall vivid details of his past life in ancient Egypt. Placed under deep hypnosis, the sculptor became Ra Ho Tep, a IVth Dynasty shaman who spoke a lost Egyptian dialect. Puharich's work with Ra Ho Tep revealed that the ancient shamanistic phenomenon of leaving the body was linked to the use of the sacred mushroom, *Aminita Muscaria*. As part of his study, Puharieh interviewed anthropologist Gordon Wasson, an expert on drug use among primitive mystics. Wasson told of an ancient mushroom cult that still existed in remote regions of the Mexican desert, in which *curanderos*, or sorcerers, ate psilocybin mushrooms in healing and divination ceremonies. Of particular interest to Carlos was the fact that Puharich had also involved Aldous Huxley in his experiments. With Huxley in attendance, Ra Ho Tep had requested and was given some sacred mushrooms, and then proceeded through the motions of an ancient ritual. Puharich's book also included conversations with anthropologist J. S. Slotkin, who specialized in the study of the Native American Church, which used peyote to reach dream states of non-ordinary reality.

These notions of non-ordinary reality appealed to Carlos. He identified strongly with the Dutch sculptor who brought forth Ra Ho Tep from his subconscious, a man named Harry Stone. Like Stone, Carlos was a foreigner in America, shy and insecure, who'd been trying to no avail for almost a decade to establish himself as an artist. The idea of never reaching his potential frightened Carlos. He often complained to Margaret about the routine sameness of his very ordinary life, how he got up every morning, went to class, went to work, came home, started over again the next day. It was not the kind of future he'd envisioned, a lifetime toting his lunch to work in a brown paper bag. There had to be something more.

And so it was that Carlos found himself in an undergraduate anthropology class called California Ethnography. Needing a topic for a term paper, he decided to continue the work of Puharich and Huxley, Wasson and Slotkin, and conduct a ethno-botanical study of the natural hallucinogenic plants of the American southwest. The professor's assignment carried an interesting caveat: anyone who actually went out into the field and found a live Indian informant would automatically receive an A.

Now, on this January evening in 1960, Carlos walked past Margaret, into the living room of her apartment, and came face to face with her gentleman caller, a wealthy Jordanian businessman she'd been seeing daily for the past two weeks, during which time Carlos had been roaming the California desert, looking for an Indian informant, hoping to secure an A, an early leg on his new career choice—professor of anthropology.

The two men chatted amiably for a few minutes, and then the subject turned to Margaret, who had resumed her place on the over-stuffed chintz sofa, next to the Jordanian. His name was Farid Aweimrine. He was the brother of another man Margaret had dated in the past; they'd met at a Christmas party. Carlos continued to stand.

"You know," said Aweimrine, "I would have married Margaret the first night I met her if my divorce had been final."

"Over my dead body!" said Carlos.

"Well why haven't you married her?" asked Farid.

Carlos looked puzzled for a moment. He crossed his arms, scratched his chin. "You know," he said wistfully, "I never thought of that." He turned to Margaret, broke a big grin. "Come on, Mayaya! We're getting married tonight!"

* * *

On a winter afternoon in 1973, Carlos and Gloria sat cross-legged on the beach near Malibu, a blanket wrapped cozily around their shoulders. The sun was low on the horizon, a blood-orange ball; wispy clouds glowed pink and magenta against the perfect cerulean sky. Seagulls swooped overhead, calling and complaining; sandpipers skittled on stick legs across the sand; surfers in wet suits worked a left-hand break a quarter mile offshore. Carlos took Gloria's hand tenderly in both of his, gazed into her startling, gold-flecked blue eyes.

"You have always been like a bird, like a little bird in a cage," he said, projecting his voice above the rush and pound of the waves. "You are wanting to fly, you're ready, the door is open—but you're just sitting there. I want to take you with me. I'll help you soar. Nothing could stop you if you come with me."

Gloria Garvin was transfixed. Though she was an attractive young woman who'd heard her share of come-on lines during her hippie wanderings of the late sixties, no one had ever spoken to her quite like this. What Carlos was saying was kind of corny, really, the sort of drivel usually reserved for the well-thumbed pages of her mother's romance novels, but somehow it didn't come across to her that way at all—somehow it was new and magical and deeply fetching. She was 26 years old, petite but amply breasted, with porcelain skin and Cleopatra bangs. She had first heard of Carlos Castaneda on a cold day in early 1969, at a long table in the dining room of an old Victorian townhouse in Haight-Ashbury. She and her boyfriend had thumbed up to San Francisco from L.A. to see the Grateful Dead at the Fillmore West. When they returned from the marathon concert, someone made a big pumpkin pie laced with hashish, and they all ate their fill—reveling in the synchronous pleasure of getting high and satisfying their munchies simultaneously. They lay around on pillows on the floor for the rest of the night, dressed in their velvets and buckskins and beads, mesmerized by the glowing light from a paper Japanese lantern that seemed to be receiving them into the universe.

The next afternoon, still pretty wasted, they were sitting around the dining room table, drinking coffee and smoking joints, when someone began reading aloud from a review of *The Teachings of Don Juan*. It was a powerful book, simply written yet deeply affecting, a groovy trip into the heady netherworld of psychedelic drugs and alternative realities—Kerouac does psychotropics. Billed as non-fiction anthropology, issued first by UCLA's University Press, and shortly thereafter by Simon and Schuster, it read more like a novel, an odd combination of Hemingway's bland staccato and Garcia-Marquez's magical realism. Regardless of its genre—about which there would eventually be much debate—the book was perfectly suited to its times, an era of sex and drugs and flower power, of back-to-the-land innocence and marvelous cosmic yearnings. Offered in the form of journal entries, the story is set in a hard scrabble desert landscape of organ pipe cacti and glittering lave massifs. It documents the weird, taxing and sometimes antic apprenticeship of a skeptical, slightly annoying young academic to a wily old Yaqui Indian sorcerer named Don Juan Matus, whom Carlos said he met through a friend in the waiting room of a Greyhound bus station, on the Arizona side of the Mexican border, approximately six months after his marriage to Margaret Runyon.

Peopled with indigenous Indians, anthropomorphic incarnations, spirits both playful and malevolent, the book evokes mysterious winds and terrifying sounds, the shiver of leaves at twilight, the loftiness of a crow in flight, the raw fragrance of tequila and the vile, fibrous taste of peyote. Carlos writes of his meetings with Mescalito, who comes to him disguised successively as a playful black dog, a column of singing light and a cricket-like being with a warty green head. He hears awesome and unexplained rumblings from dead lava hills; converses with a bilingual coyote; sews shut the eyes of a lizard with a needle and thread harvested from a cactus; meets the guardian of the Second Attestation, a hundred-foot gnat with spiky tufted hair and drooling jaws. In dry, detached, scholarly language, he details the preparation and ingestion of *humito*, the little smoke, made from the dust of psilocybin mushrooms, and of *yerba del diablo*, the devil's weed, datura, which causes his head to sprout wings and beak and feet, transform into a crow, and fly off into the heavens. At every development, Carlos remains the skeptical rationalist, a modern Everyman, trying in vain to translate his mystical experiences into the kind of concrete understanding which drives the Western mind. As such, his only tools are his questions—his persistent, often fumbling effort to keep up a Socratic dialogue with Don Juan:

"Did I take off like a bird?" he asks the old sorcerer, upon awakening from an experience with the devil's weed, one of twenty-two drug trips in the first two books.

"You always ask me questions I cannot answer," the old man tells him. "What you want to know makes no sense. Birds fly like birds and a man who has taken the devil's weed flies as such."

Beneath the spectral fireworks and psychedelic drama in *The Teachings* (and in the subsequent eleven volumes that would follow over the course of the next 30 years) is Carlos's quest to become a Warrior, a Man of Knowledge wholly at one with his environment. Agile and strong, unencumbered by sentiment or personal history, the Warrior knows that each act may be his last. He is alone. Death is the root of his life, and in its constant presence the Warrior always performs "impeccably." He is attuned to the desert, to its sounds and shadows, its animals and birds, its power spots and holes of refuge. The Warrior's aim in becoming a Man of Knowledge, the young academic learns through his apprenticeship, is "to stop the world" and "see"—to experience life directly, grasping its essence without interpreting it, coming eventually to the realization that the universe, as perceived by everyday humans, is just a construct based on shared customs and languages and understandings.

In truth, Don Juan tells his bumbling and often frightened student, men and women are not flesh at all. They are made up of fine fibers of light, glowing white cobwebs that stretch from the head to the navel, forming an egg of circulating threads, with arms and legs of luminous bristles bursting in all directions. Through a series of long fibers that shoot out from the center of the abdomen, every man and woman is joined with every other man and woman, and with his surroundings, and with the universe. Don Juan lectures Carlos: "a man is a luminous egg whether he's a beggar or a king and there's no way to change anything." Of particular import in this cosmic anatomy is the Assemblage Point, a place of intense luminosity, located about an arm's length behind the shoulder blades, where perception takes place. By shifting or displacing the assemblage point during dream states, the old Nagual taught, a practitioner could gain entrance into other worlds, something called "The Art of Dreaming."

When Gloria returned to L.A., flush with the new possibilities of Don Juan's worlds, she mentioned the far-out book to her aunt, who was working in the graduate research library at UCLA. The married author, it turned out, haunted the grad library, particularly the rare book room. He was also dating a library worker the aunt knew well. In short order, a meeting was arranged.

Gloria and her boyfriend spent the whole afternoon with the great man in the student union at UCLA. Sitting at a Formica table, amid the hectic bustle of the student body, they spoke about life and death, drugs and sex, meaning and shamanism. At the end of their time together, Carlos took Gloria's hand for the first time. "This was a most auspicious meeting," he said. Then he nodded his head in the direction of her boyfriend. "Too bad you brought that nincompoop along with you."

Over the next few years, Gloria and Carlos stayed in touch by letter and by phone. At his urging, she enrolled in UCLA as an undergraduate anthropology student. Later, also at his urging, she broke off her longstanding engagement to her boyfriend.

Carlos, meanwhile, published his second book, *A Separate Reality: Further Conversations with Don Juan*, and then his third, *Journey to Ixlan: The Lessons of Don Juan*, which served simultaneously as his doctoral thesis.

In a departure from the first two volumes, Carlos revealed in *Ixlan* that the drug part of the program was now over. After ten years of study with the old Indian, he wrote in the Introduction to *Ixlan*, "It became evident to me that my original assumption about the role of psychotropic plants was erroneous. They were not the essential feature of the sorcerer's description of the world, but were only an aid to cement, so to speak, parts of the description which I had been incapable of perceiving otherwise. My insistence on holding on to my standard version of reality rendered me almost deaf and blind to Don Juan's aims. Therefore, it was simply my lack of sensitivity which has fostered their use." Now that his eyes had been properly opened, he wrote, it was necessary to focus on what the old sorcerer had called the "techniques for stopping the world." Only then could he become an impeccable Warrior.

"One needs the mood of a warrior for every single act," Don Juan tells him in typical fashion, harsh and judgmental but also loving. "Otherwise one becomes distorted and ugly. There is no power in a life that lacks this mood. Look at yourself. Everything offends and upsets you. You whine and complain and feel that everyone is making you dance to their tune.... A warrior, on the other hand, is a hunter. He calculates everything. That's control. But once his calculations are over, he acts. He lets go. That's abandon. A warrior is not a leaf at the mercy of the wind. No one can push him; no one can make him do things against himself or against his better judgment. A warrior is trained to survive, and he survives in the best of all possible fashions."

As it was, by the time his third book was published, Carlos's notion of survival had taken on quite a different hue. By 1973, he had become nothing short of a cult figure; would-be disciples and counter-culture tourists were flocking to Mexico, combing the deserts for mushrooms and Don Juan. *The Teachings* was selling an astounding 16,000 copies a week. *Ixlan* was a hardback best-seller. Sales of the paperback made Carlos a millionaire. He traded in his old VW bus for a new Audi, bought the compound on Pandora in Westwood Village. Before long, *Time* came calling.

In what would be his first and last major interview, Carlos told *Time* that he was born to a well-known family in São Paulo, Brazil, on Christmas Day, 1935. At the time of his birth, he said, his father, who would later become a professor of literature, was 17. His mother was 15. He was raised by his maternal grandparents on a chicken farm until he was six, at which point his parents took custody. The happy reunion was cut short, however, when his mother died. The doctor's diagnosis, Carlos told *Time*, was pneumonia, but he believed the cause had been acedia, a condition of numbed inertia. "She was morose, very beautiful and dissatisfied; an ornament," he told *Time*. "My despair was that I wanted to make her something else, but how could she listen to me? I was only six."

Carlos was left to be raised by his father, a shadowy figure whom he mentions in the books with a mixture of fondness, pity and contempt. His father's weakness of will, he told *Time*, was the obverse to the "impeccability" of Don Juan. In the books, Carlos describes his father's efforts to become a writer as a farce of indecision. He told *Time*: "I am my father. Before I met Don Juan I would spend years sharpening my pencils and then getting a headache every time I sat down to write. Don Juan taught me that that's stupid. If you want to do something, do it impeccably, and that's all that matters."

Carlos was educated, he told *Time*, at a "very proper" boarding school in Buenos Aires, where he acquired the Spanish (he already spoke Italian and Portuguese) in which he would later interview Don Juan. At 15, he said, he became so unmanageable that an uncle, the family patriarch—Carlos told people he was Oswaldo Aranha, a legendary gaucho and revolutionary who would later become president of Brazil—had him placed with a foster family in Los Angeles. The year was 1951. He enrolled in Hollywood High School. Graduating two years later, he went overseas to study sculpture at the Academy of Fine Arts in Milan, only to discover that "I did not have the sensitivity or the openness to be a great artist." Dispirited, he returned to Los Angeles and enrolled at UCLA. "I really threw my life out the window. I said to myself: if it's going to work, it must be new," he told *Time* of his resolve to take up anthropology. In 1959, he told the magazine, he changed his name to Castaneda.

"Thus Castaneda's own biography," concluded *Time*, "creates an elegant consistency—the spirited young man moving from his academic background in an exhausted, provincial European culture toward revitalization by the shaman; the gesture of abandoning the past to disentangle himself from crippling memories. Unfortunately, it is largely untrue."

In short order, the reporter for *Time* came up with a radically different account of Carlos's early life, a story later confirmed and appended by Castaneda scholar Richard DeMille, the adopted son of movie mogul Cecil B. DeMille, who has made a life's work of studying Carlos.

According to U.S. immigration records, Carlos César Salvador Arana Castaneda entered the U.S. at San Francisco in 1951, at the age of 26. He became a naturalized U.S. citizen in 1959. He was born in Peru, in the ancient Inca town of Cajamarca, where witches and *curanderos* were not at all uncommon in the town marketplace. Carlos was the son of a watchmaker and goldsmith named César Arana Burungary, who owned a jewelry shop in the downtown section of the city and was himself the son of an Italian immigrant. Once a promising student, his father was known during his youth as a Bohemian who squandered his academic opportunities after falling in with a fast crowd of artists and bullfighters in the capital city of Lima. Settling down at last to family life as an artisan and shopkeeper, he was a tireless chess player, a constant reader of Kant and Spinoza. His mother was a slender, almond-eyed girl of 16 named Susana Castaneda Novoa.

She died when Carlos was 24. He refused to attend the funeral, according to a cousin, and locked himself in his room for three days without eating. When he emerged from his mourning, he declared his intention to go to America.

In his youth, Carlos was an altar boy, attended the local pubic school. He often went with his father to the jewelry shop; over time he became skilled in working with copper and gold, but he hated selling the things he made. After dropping out of school in Cajamarca, Carlos moved to Lima, where he finished high school and then enrolled in Bellas Artes, Peru's national academy of fine arts. A former roommate remembers Carlos as "a big liar and a real friend," a witty fellow who loved carousing but never drank or smoked, who made a living playing cards, horses and dice while harboring "like an obsession" to go to the United States and become rich from gambling. A former classmate recalled Carlos as "a very capable fellow, likable and rather mysterious. A first class seducer. I remember the girls used to spend the morning waiting around for him at the Bellas Artes. We called him The Smile of Gold because he had, I think, a gold tooth. Sometimes he would go to the market with some used watches which he could only make run for two or three hours. He would sell the watches and then disappear... He was always thinking up unlikely stories—tremendous, beautiful things. At times he sold blankets and ponchos from the mountains."

Confronted by the reporter from *Time*, Carlos was characteristically unfazed: "To ask me to verify my life by giving you my statistics is like using science to validate sorcery," he said. "It robs the world of its magic."

More alarming, perhaps, than the murkiness of Carlos's history, was the debate that raged over the academic veracity of his work. Billed as ethnography, it read like a novel and sold like a best-seller—the envy, no doubt, of many a scholar who had worked in the trenches of anthropology for a lifetime. Though the panel of professors at UCLA who awarded his doctorate continued to stand firmly behind him—in an introduction to *The*

Teachings, one of them lauds Carlos for "his patience, his courage, and his perspicacity"—social scientists were skeptical, labeling the work a fictionalized composite in the guise of anthropology, a dramatic rehash that borrowed heavily from the work of others at the expense of accuracy and truth, not to mention credit.

In his two volumes on Carlos, DeMille collected ample evidence of what he considered a fraud. Citing myriad examples large and small, he made a case that Carlos's books were nothing more than cleverly conceived and masterfully executed works of fiction. Among hundreds of well-researched nits, DeMille pointed to the facts that, over his years of apprenticeship to the old Indian, Carlos never learned the Indian names for any of the plants or animals he comes into contact with, and neither did Carlos ever submit a specimen of Don Juan's mushrooms for chemical testing. DeMille quoted experts—Wasson among them—who said that hallucinogenic mushrooms do not, in fact, grow in the Sonoran desert, and that the practice of smoking mushroom powder was unknown prior to Carlos's books. According to Wasson, the godfather of such studies, mushrooms are more usually eaten or brewed into tea, and even when allowed to dry, they normally macerate into shreds, rather than into a powder. In any case, he said the leavings do not burn.

Though much of the story takes place in the desert, an expert on climatology—writing in DeMille's second book, a collection of essays and interviews debunking Carlos's work—said that desert conditions, during the times of year Carlos describes, would have been harsh and impassable. In one of Carlos's entries, for example, dated in August, Carlos writes of hiking to the top of a hill at noon-time "to rest in the open unshaded area until dusk." In another entry, dated in June, he describes the evening wind as being "cold." Summer temperatures in the Sonoran desert are typically as high as 120 degrees by noon. At night, they hover around 100.

Moreover, throughout their extensive desert travels, Carlos and Don Juan went unmolested by the kind of pests and predators—scorpions, rattlesnakes, swarming saguaro fruit flies, razor-toothed desert javelinas—that normally torment hikers. He never mentions some of the more colorful inhabitants of the desert—nine-inch centipedes, tarantulas as big as saucers, gila monsters, chuckawallas and horned toads. During his adventures, Carlos writes of climbing high trees. Yet the trees in the desert—*palo verde*, ironwood, mesquite—are nearly impossible to climb, and neither are they high. Their branches tangle into thorny thickets. Higher than six feet they are too weak to climb. Carlos catches five quails at once in a hastily assembled trap. He runs down a jackrabbit and snares it with his bare hands. He hurdles breakneck and terrified through the desert, through barrel cacti and prickly pears and thorny scrub bushes, but never once does he mention being stabbed or cut by thorns. And while he wrote in his books that he took notes on everything—his note-taking, in fact, becomes an object of derision by Don Juan and his associates—Carlos never produced any field notes.

A close reading of Carlos's books, said DeMille and his collected experts, revealed Don Juan's teachings to be an amalgamation of American Indian folklore, oriental mysticism, and European philosophy—drawing on, among others, Huxley and Puharich, Slotkin and Wasson, Goddard and Yogi Ramacharaka, a pseudonymous American whose works are still widely available in occult bookstores.

Of equal concern was the existence of Don Juan himself. According to Carlos, the old Nagual was born in 1891, watched his parents murdered by soldiers, suffered through the government-forced diaspora of the Yaquis all over Mexico during that era. DeMille and his experts point out that while many Indian tribes, such as the Huichols, use peyote rituals, the Yaquis, as a rule, did not. Yaqui sorcerers, they continued, don't take apprentices, either. It didn't help matters that not one known expert on the desert culture of the Southwest had ever heard anything about Don Juan and his party. Or that exhaustive attempts to locate the wily old Indian were unsuccessful. In *Carlos Castaneda,*

Academic Opportunism and the Psychedelic Sixties, anthropologist Jay Courtney Fikes posits that Don Juan was a composite of a number of different shamans who'd been discovered, variously, by Wasson and by several of Carlos's colleagues in the anthropology department at UCLA. Indeed: Why else would a field researcher spend so much time in UCLA's graduate research library?

"Although Castaneda's concocted episodes often have something authentic about them, they trivialize Huichol, Yaqui or any Native American culture..." writes Fikes. "Those few kernels of truth Castaneda's books contain are dissolved inside a concoction full of spurious ingredients. Finding ethnographic truth in Castaneda's books is almost as laborious as panning for gold."

Even while debunking him, however, DeMille exhibited a fondness and a overarching respect for Carlos and his work. The continuing saga might have been the product of Carlos's mind—but what a marvelous saga it was, what a valuable mind:

"Castaneda wasn't a common con man, he lied to bring us the truth," DeMille wrote in his first book, *Castaneda's Journey.* "His stories are packed with truth, though they are not true stories, which he said they are. This is not your familiar literary allegorist painlessly instructing his readers in philosophy. Nor is it your fearless trustworthy ethnographer returned full of anecdotes from the forests of Ecuador. This is a sham-man bearing gifts, an ambiguous spellbinder dealing simultaneously in contrary commodities—wisdom and deception."

After the meeting in the student union, it would be four years before Gloria Garvin actually saw Carlos again face to face. Meanwhile, she read all his books, followed all the publicity, participated in the gossip that was rampant in the anthro department at UCLA. Part of the gossip centered around Carlos's very earthly reputation as a Lothario. Some even questioned whether he ever went to the desert at all—his wanderings, they said, were just a ruse to cover his bed hopping. Besides the library worker—who, he would later claim, was energetically damaged during her own studies with Don Juan and would live with him in the Pandora compound for many years—Carlos was also involved with two women in the department, Regine Thal and Ann Marie Carter, who would later change their names to Florinda Donner-Grau and Taisha Abelar. He also began seeing a married mother of two named Judy Guilford, who would later call herself Beverly Ames, and then eventually Carol Tiggs. Tiggs would become especially famous in Castaneda circles as a powerful sorceress who crossed over into the Second Attention for ten years and then returned to help guide Carlos and the others in his inner circle. Together, Tiggs, Donner-Grau and Abelar would form the triumvirate of Witches who surrounded Carlos for the duration of his life. All three would write books about their own, separate apprenticeships with Don Juan.

Gloria talked to Carlos now and then by phone, exchanged the occasional letter, but never saw him in person until one day, walking across campus during the winter quarter of 1973, she spotted him. Their eyes locked, he came over. He acted as if they'd met only yesterday.

And so it was that Carlos and Gloria were sitting cross-legged on the beach at sunset, a blanket wrapped cozily around their shoulders. He had her hand clasped tenderly in both of his; he gazed deeply into her startling, gold-flecked blue eyes. "What this entails is not a normal relationship," he told her. "I want to take you with me but it won't be as a normal man, because I am not a normal man any longer. I want to take care of you. I want you to be my wife. I've always known that. Don Juan has told me that. He's seen you; you've hovered around me in dreams. He has identified you as the woman who is going to be in the center of the hurricane with me. There are other winds in the north, south, east and west, and they are very cold and ruthless women, but you are not that way. I want to take care of you. I will do everything in my power for you, because this is a commitment, one that has existed for a very long time. One that will exist beyond this lifetime."

With that Carlos leaned over and kissed Gloria. It was an intense, directed sort of kiss; not passionate, not sloppy, not out of control, just very directed, she can't describe it any other way. At that moment, the sounds of the beach grew silent. Time stood still. She felt herself giving something away to him, something very deep, something of herself she'd never reclaim.

* * *

Fast asleep on a futon in his modest apartment, late one night in the spring of 1985, a 32-year-old computer technician named Jeremy Davidson found himself on a mountain top, wearing nothing but his underwear.

He was standing on a rocky ridge, at the edge of a sheer cliff. Eagles soared, riding the updrafts. Clouds floated past; wispy fingers of moisture caressed his face. Beneath him, hundreds of feet below, was a gorgeous clear lake. He turned slowly in all directions, inhaling the crisp air, taking in the view, trying to form a clear and lasting image of the whole place, performing a systematic intake, the way Don Juan recommended. It was a wondrous alpine setting, with craggy escarpments and evergreen trees, snowcaps on the distant peaks. Though it was cold and windy, he was comfortable and warm, filled with a buoyant sense of well-being despite his precarious barefoot perch. A feeling of giddiness overcame him and he took off running—hopping and skipping from boulder to boulder like an astronaut bounding across the surface of the moon. Changing direction, he plunged straight down the cliff face, pausing here and there to flip and spin and twirl, throwing tricks like a free-style ski-jumper, making his way toward the languid blue waters of the lake.

The scene changed and he was standing in a small cove, his toes buried in fine, gritty sand. Thinking it might help to cement the dream, to make it last longer, he decided to look at his hands for a bit. He sat down in the sand, concentrated on his palms, his fingers, his nails. Just then, a big wave rose up and washed over him, enveloping him in bubbles and blue, sending him sprawling.

Rising to his feet, Jeremy moved toward the back of the cove, toward a trail. He walked for a while through the dense woods, then came upon a building in a clearing, a huge Hansel and Gretel type affair, a gingerbread house with fancy trim. He got the feeling it was an abandoned resort hotel. He decided to explore.

The scene changed again and he was inside, in the lobby, a room with a fireplace and overstuffed chairs, a gift shop off to one side, cobwebs and dust everywhere. As he looked around, performing a systematic intake, things seemed to become more and more solid, as if he was watching an image download from the web onto a computer screen. He walked into the gift shop, helped himself to a dry T-shirt that was hanging conveniently on a rack. Off to one side, behind the cash register, he saw an opening, like a door, leading into a blue-green world. He stood a moment, regarding the opening, trying to decide what to do next. Then he spoke aloud: "I intend to go to where the sorcerers are. Take me to the sorcerers...."

Shy and highly intelligent, a bit at odds with the world, Jeremy Davidson had first discovered the writings of Carlos Castaneda in the late seventies, while studying physics as a college junior. He'd always been a seeker, a skeptic, a bit of an outsider, the kind of person for whom the normal order and the normal answers never seemed to ring true. He'd experimented with psychedelic drugs, read extensively on eastern and western philosophy. He'd been a Buddhist and a Scientologist, an atheist and an orthodox Jew. More recently, during a bad period in his life he'd re-discovered Carlos. Starting with *The Teachings*, he'd worked his way through the series, which had grown by now to eight books.

Carlos himself had long since disappeared from the public eye. Smarting, no doubt, from the effects of his exposure in the early seventies, he lived in quiet anonymity in the Pandora compound with the Witches, traveling around the country and to Mexico, churning out books all the while, honing the message and the method, taking it further with each new publication. Though Carlos said that Don Juan left the world in 1973, dying "the immaculate death" of the Warrior, each subsequent book continued to expound upon Don Juan's teachings. Diligent readers noted that the anthropological references seemed to grow fewer as the series progressed, and that the books increasingly bore the traces of other influences, such as phenomenology, Eastern mysticism and existentialism. With Don Juan having left the world, Carlos himself became the heir to the sorcerer's lineage, the Nagual. No longer a disciple, he had become the prophet. As the books evolved, his focus turned more and more toward the Art of Dreaming.

According to Carlos, Don Juan was an intermediary between the natural world of everyday life and an unseen universe called the Second Attention. Though Western minds are conditioned to believe that the world we live in is unique and absolute, it is, in truth, only one in a cluster of consecutive worlds, arranged like the layers of an onion. Don Juan said that even though humans have been energetically conditioned to perceive only their own world, they still have the capability to enter those other realms—worlds as palpable, unique, absolute and engulfing as the ordinary reality that we live in every day.

Don Juan said that in order for people to visit those other realms—the existence of which are constant and independent of our awareness—they had to first recondition their energetic capacity to perceive. To this end, he prescribed a series of techniques designed to displace the Assemblage Point, a place of intense luminosity, located about an arm's length behind the shoulder blades, where perception occurs, where we receive the signals that tell us what we see, feel, hear and understand. Furthermore, said Don Juan, once a person became adept at traveling to the Second Attention, he or she could ultimately remain there as a luminous egg for all of eternity, in a wonderful universe too vast and beautiful and complex and fulfilling to render in conventional language or ideas.

Reading all of this, Jeremy felt invigorated and alive, perhaps more so than he'd ever been in his whole life. Here, at last, was a belief system that felt right to him. It was a system that stressed living every moment to the fullest, as a Warrior and a Man of Knowledge, rising to every trial as a challenge, taking responsibility for everything you have a part in, living impeccably every single day. And, it was a system that explained the place of man in the universe, and the nature of that universe itself. Added to all of this was the promise of other worlds, not just worlds you could visit in an afterlife, but worlds you could visit right now, today. In sum, the Sorcerer's Way was a mode of thinking as well as a mode of acting—a world view that offered its adherents not only ideas and guidelines but also procedures and results. You didn't just sit around believing. You could act.

Jeremy thus embarked on the path of the impeccable Warrior. He sought to live each day as a challenge, as a discipline. He strove to eliminate self-importance, to use death as an advisor, to erase personal history, to disrupt the routines of his life. He tried to have a romance with knowledge, and to write people he cared about a blank check of affection. He practiced gazing and not doing, stalking and the right way of walking. He tried to stop the world and to see. He watched for omens and read infinity, a specific gazing technique where he focused on a fixed point until a violet field appeared, then continued to focus until a little blotch of pomegranate exploded into either written words or visual scenes. He spent hours recapitulating his life—a laborious process in which he reviewed each and every contact he'd ever had with another human being since his first memories after birth, an effort to regain wasted energy. Slowly but surely, he began to become aware in his dreams—he began traveling to the Second Attention.

Now Jeremy found himself in a gift shop somewhere in the mountains, having entered the Second Attention from his futon one night in the spring of 1985. He walked through a doorway into a blue green world, intending to go to the Sorcerers.

As he entered the doorway, a force that he had come to think of as The Spirit picked him up and flew him over a vast area like a huge town square, filled with thousands of people. From his vantage point high in the sky, he could look down and see their faces. Most of them, he could see, were in some state of fear, degradation, agony. Some of them looked up as he soared past. Again he voiced his intent: "I intend to go to where the Sorcerers are."

The scene changed and he found himself on the ground in a dark, smoky gray area. There were small, dark beings surrounding him, and when he focused on them, they turned to face him. They were ghoul-like creatures, with yellowish eyes and a single protuberance extending out from their faces, terminating in creepy little mouths. They began advancing.

Retreating, he entered another area, inhabited by a different sort of beings, tall blocks of dark shadows, like huge sentient rectangles. They too began to surround him, and he found himself standing on something that looked like a gray tombstone lying flat on the ground. Scared of the beings, wishing to leave, he knelt down and clenched his fist, placed it upon the stone. "I want to go where the Chacmols are," he said out loud, but nothing happened. He was about to repeat his demand, using the name of one of the Witches, Taisha Abelar, when a voice told him not to do that, but rather to restate his intention. This time he said firmly: " I INTEND to go to where the Chacmols are."

With that, the scene changed and he was in a cave, with rock floors and walls and boulders strewn everywhere. Though there was no source of light apparent, it was bright as day. He walked around the cave, exploring. Suddenly a man jumped out from behind a rock. He was primitive, vigorous, wild looking, wearing fur clothes. He ran towards Jeremy; Jeremy turned and fled. The caveman chased him through a vast system of tunnels and caverns, gaining with every step, getting closer and closer. Just as the caveman was about to overtake him, Jeremy spotted a hole. It seemed to lead into another chamber. He dove through.

The scene changed and he was flying again, in a prone position with his arms extended like Superman. He felt his mood lighten; up up up he sailed, high into the sky, toward the moon, bright and full. He made a smooth banking turn and headed back toward earth, toward a shopping mall. In his mind, he considered leaving this place, flying out toward the countryside somewhere, but the voice inside his head overruled his thoughts and The Spirit took control of his flight, as it sometimes did, and he began to descend. He flew into the mall, around the atrium, past a fountain and an escalator.

The scene changed. He was inside of a store, a sex shop. There was racy lingerie hanging on the racks, all kinds of toys on the shelves. Drawn to the toys, he was about to pick one up when he noticed a bunch of people in a back room, men and women in various states of undress, an orgy in progress. He stood for a few minutes and watched. A man came over with his attractive girlfriend. He offered her to Jeremy. Though his inner voice clearly told him "No!", Jeremy ignored the voice and took the girl in his arms, began pulling off the remainder of her clothes. She seemed a bit reluctant. Jeremy got the strong impression that she'd never done this sort of thing before, that she was only doing it to please her boyfriend. It bothered him a bit that maybe she wasn't totally into the whole scene, but she was beautiful; it had been a long time since he'd been with a woman. The voice told him No! He reached for her breast....

He awoke in his futon. He sat up, feeling a bit ashamed. He had not acted like a Warrior. He shouldn't have crossed the wishes of the inner voice. He shouldn't have defied The Spirit. It was months before he dreamed again.

* * *

At precisely 9 a.m. on Christmas Eve, 1993—the same time as every morning for the past several months—the phone rang in Melissa Ward's Santa Monica apartment. She was in bed with a horrible flu; she just wanted to be alone. The phone rang again, then again. The shrill noise hurt her head. Finally, she picked it up.

"How's my baby girl?" sang Carlos.

"Still pretty sick, I'm afraid."

"You're coming to the dinner tonight, aren't you?"

"I don't know, Carlos," she said, and then she sighed. "I feel like I've been run over by a truck."

"But you have to be there! The whole dinner is for you!"

She rolled her eyes toward the ceiling. They were a startling shade of cornflower blue, with gold flecks that shimmered in the light. "I guess I'll have to see how I feel."

"Why don't I come over and bring you some chicken soup?"

"No no no!" she said quickly. "Don't bother. Really! I'll be okay."

"Well you have to rest," insisted Carlos. "Don't go to work, don't do anything, just rest. You have to be ready. Tonight, you become one of us!"

"Well, er, um," said Melissa, pushing her Cleopatra bangs away from her forehead. He'd been talking about this mysterious dinner for weeks now. Frankly, it gave her the creeps. *Become one of us!* The way he said it made her shudder. It had the distinct ring of something cult-like; she didn't like the sound of it, not at all. "I'm gonna try my best to make it," she said half-heartedly.

"You must make it!" roared Carlos. "Everything is ready. You are the Electric Warrior! We have been searching for you for all of eternity! We have found you just in the nick of time. You must come!"

Thirty-eight years old, petite and attractive, Melissa Ward was born beneath the Northern Lights at a secret military base in the Aleutian chain. Though she was a bit too young to have been a hippie, she grew up with her feet planted firmly in the early seventies counter-culture, into eastern religions and Credence Clearwater Revival, psychedelics, the writings of Gurdjieff and Huxley. She was 18 when she first read Carlos. She'd just returned from backpacking through Europe; she was severely ill with colitis, in a lot of pain, trying to cure herself naturally with herbs. Staying by herself in a friend's cabin in the woods, lying around naked, trying to fight the sickness, she came upon a copy of *Journey to Ixlan* on a shelf. She opened the book at random, let her eyes drift down the page. "Death is always following you," she read. In her condition, the words rang very true. She turned to the front of the book and started in.

Melissa had been reading for an hour or two when she heard some weird scratching noises outside. She struggled out of bed, looked through the window. There, on the deck, was a giant black bird, the biggest crow she'd ever seen. It was hopping up and down, acting very strangely, like it was trying to get her attention. Stranger still was the fact that crows played a significant part in *Ixlan*. In Don Juan's world, crows were said to be the incarnations of powerful sorcerers and spirits. Under the influence of the devil's weed, Carlos himself had become a crow—his head had sprouted wings, a bill and feet and had flown off into the heavens. Over the next few days, as she continued reading the book, the crow became bolder. It tapped on the window with its beak, hopped from place to place on the deck, knocked over little pots of herbs, generally making itself known. By the third day, her curiosity got the better of her and she ventured out to the deck, sat down with her new companion. The crow hopped up on her chair. She fed it grapes. Though she might have been delirious, she could have sworn the crow had a kind of benevolent presence. In an odd, unexplainable way, it seemed to be there for her, to help her through this rough time. The crow visited every day for a month, until she was fully recovered. Then it disappeared.

Time passed and she went on with her life, forgot all about Carlos. After bouncing around from job to job, she enrolled as an undergraduate at UCLA. By her junior year, in the winter of 1993, her life was full and hectic, more gratifying than ever. She was working part time as a nutrition consultant, writing for the college newspaper, doing an internship at the actress Jessica Lange's film company, taking a full load of classes—looking forward, meanwhile, to graduation and the promise of a job in either journalism or entertainment. And then one day she got a phone call from her mom. She was dying of cancer.

The next nine months were a living hell. Melissa nursed her mom to the end, held her hand as she took her last breath, sat alone with the body for three hours until the man from the funeral home came to take her. Melissa handled all of the arrangements, served as executor of the will. Trying to get back to her life, she enrolled in summer school, only to find herself embroiled in a disastrous affair with her older, married creative writing teacher. By the end of the summer she'd dropped out of school and taken to her bed in a deep depression. Lying beneath the covers with the shades drawn, she repeated to herself a manta of despair: "Nobody cares. I've given up hope. Life sucks."

Then one day in September, she ran into a friend at the health food store. He said he was going to another friend's apartment to hear Carlos Castaneda speak to a small group. The session had been arranged primarily through the efforts of a German woman named Gabi Geuther, a New Age enthusiast and veteran of primal scream therapy who'd befriended Florinda Donner-Grau and other members of the inner circle after a reading at a women's bookstore in Santa Monica. For the first time in many years, Melissa thought of the weird and friendly crow who'd helped her through hard times. She decided to come along.

Though Melissa didn't realize it just then, the fact that Carlos had begun to appear in public after a 20-year absence signaled a stunning change in direction for the Nagual and his party. Over the last few years, they'd slowly begun taking on select students for a weekly private class, held in a rented room in a dance studio. Now, apparently, they'd decided to rev things up, to actively promote the ideas and practices of Don Juan on a larger scale, to make them available for public consumption. To this end, Carlos and the Witches had hired a lawyer and formed several corporations, with the stated intent of establishing "a magical relationship between the endeavors of a corporate unit in our modern world and the purpose and will of a bygone era." Toltec Artists was a management agency—run by inner-circle member Tracy Kramer, a well-known Hollywood agent—set up to handle the literary careers of Carlos, the three Witches, and assorted other connected artists. Laugan Productions was a company that sold instructional videos and other saleable products. Most important was Cleargreen, which acted as both a publishing house and as the sponsor of seminars and workshops for something they were now billing as Carlos Castaneda's Tensegrity.

Derived from the words tension and integrity, Tensegrity was said to be a modernized version of the "magical passes" that were developed by ancient Indian shamans and passed down secretly through 27 generations to Don Juan and then to Carlos and the Witches. By practicing these exercises, Carlos said, Toltec sorcerers had attained an increased level of awareness which allowed them to perform "indescribable feats of perception" and experience "unequaled states of physical prowess and well being." Through the use of the Tensegrity exercises—a sort of combination of martial arts, meditation, yoga and aerobics—modern practitioners could achieve a new level of vigor, health and clarity. And they could gain the kind of energy needed to displace the Assemblage Point and actively engage in the Art of Dreaming, traveling at will to other worlds. While it was earlier believed that the Sorcerer's Way was a solitary pursuit, Carlos now said that the "mass" created by a group of people practicing together caused quicker and more powerful results.

Though Carlos had never before mentioned the "magical passes" in his writings; though other anthropologists insisted that there was no such tradition of body movements among pre-Hispanic Indians; and though Carlos had always eschewed the notion of selling his techniques through expensive seminars, it was Cleargreen's express purpose to disseminate the teachings of Don Juan to a large audience at a high price. What had caused the change of heart was not exactly clear. Perhaps, some suggested, Carlos saw fertile ground in the national obsessions with physical fitness and New Age philosophy—theirs was one heck of a product, a time-saving two-fer, designed to benefit both the mind and the body. Perhaps, some suggested, Carlos was becoming infirm and out of touch and the Witches had begun to call the shots.

Carlos himself acknowledged that Don Juan had always said that the magical passes should be kept secret. This new path, Carlos explained, had been spurred by an extraordinary event. According to Carlos, while following Don Juan's techniques, Carol Tiggs, one of the three Witches, had disappeared from a hotel room in Mexico City into the Second Attention. She had vanished for ten years, Carlos said, in order to act as a beacon from the other side, guiding initiates through the "dark sea of awareness." In 1985, however, Tiggs made a surprising reappearance at a California bookshop where Carlos was giving a talk. Her return had convinced Carlos that the "message of freedom" enshrined in the magical passes should now be passed onto the world at large.

Others had a more cynical view: "Castaneda had built himself up as a prophet through the Don Juan books," said anthropologist Courtney Jay Fikes. "The bible, so to speak, was written; but there was no ritual, so it was necessary to invent one."

Over the next several years, dozens of seminars—some lasting a weekend, some as long as three weeks—would be attended by thousands of Carlos enthusiasts in the U.S., Mexico and Europe. The seminars cost from $200 to $1,000. Tables were set up to sell Tensegrity T-shirts (The Magic is in the Movement) and Tensegrity videos, which had been directed by the well-known novelist and screenwriter Bruce Wagner. Also on sale were Tensegrity tools, for use in concert with the magical passes. "The Device to Enhance Centers of Awareness," was two balls made of Teflon reinforced by a ceramic compound. "The Device for Inner Silence" was a round, weighted leather-covered object for placement on the stomach. "The Wheel of Time" was invented by the Blue Scout; it was a flat disk made of compact foam rubber, extremely pliable, but durable enough to withstand pushing, pulling and twisting. Carlos himself appeared at all the early seminars; both he and the Witches gave long, amusing, passionate speeches. Interspersed with the lectures were Tensegrity demonstrations by the Chacmols, dressed in matching black workout uniforms.

Also over the next several years, serious questions would be raised about the origins of Tensegrity. Some alleged that Carlos's magical passes were nothing more than the appropriated teachings of a kung fu instructor and "energy master" named Howard Lee, with whom Carlos had studied for many years, and to whom *Ixlan* had been dedicated. Though there were allegations that Carlos paid a substantial sum of money and the phallus of a puma to deter the Santa Monica-based Lee from taking legal action against Cleargreen, Lee denied this. Smiling inscrutably, he refuses to speculate upon the actual origins of Tensegrity. He does acknowledge, however, that once Carlos began teaching Tensegrity, the formerly close relations between the two wise men become chilly.

And so, on a balmy night in September 1993, Melissa found herself among a group of 40 people, jammed into an apartment in Santa Monica, listening to the great man speak. Though she'd brought a notebook and had started out taking notes, she quickly gave up. There seemed to be no rhyme or reason to what Carlos was saying, no outline to his talk, just a torrential downpour of ideas and stories and jokes. Though she was frustrated at first, she found herself settling into her seat on the plush pile carpet and letting his words rush over her, concentrating not so much on what he was saying as on his energy. He had about him a really nice emanation, she felt, a nice kind of presence that was warm and fluid, almost like floating around in a Jacuzzi with all the jets on. Whatever this was, it was cool. She felt better than she had for months.

Carlos rambled for two hours, and when he finished he received a standing ovation. Melissa just sat there, kind of stunned. Before she knew what was happening, Carlos was standing over her. He leaned down, whispered in her ear: "You have very good energy," he said. Then he was gone.

Then next day, Melissa was contacted by one of the Chacmols, who invited her to a private class, and she went, and Carlos seated her front and center, seemed to be lecturing only to her. The next day, one of the Chacmols called to ask if Carlos might have the privilege of calling her at home. Soon, Carlos was telephoning every morning at nine a.m. sharp, sometimes late in the evening as well. He called her his baby girl. He asked her about her life, her family, her past sex life, her history of venereal disease. He told her that if she smoked pot, she should stop, and that she must completely stop having sex. "You must zip it up! You must not let anyone touch your baby-thing," he'd said. He asked her to tell him her innermost secrets; he asked her to make a list of all her sex partners, to recapitulate each experience. He asked her if she'd ever "been taken away kicking and screaming by men in white coats." Frequently, he'd ask her to lunch or dinner, for sushi or Cuban, his favorites. Usually, she said no. On those occasions when she relented and said yes, one of the Chacmols invariably would call and cancel at the last minute, telling her that Carlos was sick or that he had to leave town unexpectedly. Though they never met alone outside the weekly private classes, Carlos continued to call each morning. He told her that her energy was incredible, that they were soulmates, that he would never leave her. Melissa didn't know what to make of his attentions. Though his tone was distinctly sexual, he never made a move. It was like he had an obsessive need to make women fall in love with him, then to keep them at arm's length. While she had no interest in him sexually, his attentions were oddly addictive—she kept coming back for more, despite her better judgment.

In time, Carlos began telling Melissa that she was the Electric Warrior that they'd been searching for, and on Christmas

Eve, 1993, they held a special banquet in her honor. Though she was creeped out by the notion of what seemed to be happening, she attended the dinner, a classy affair for 18 people with champagne and candlelight at a long table in the banquet room of a four star French restaurant in Westwood. There were toasts and speeches and each of the Witches came in turn to sit next to her and chat. Though the Witches struck her as being very catty and a bit hostile—asking her, for example, what her favorite kind of music was and then berating her for her answer—she got the feeling like she was the bride at a wedding, albeit a bride who was marrying into a family who had mixed emotions about the union. With dread, she sat at the table—Carlos at one head, Florinda at the other—imagining a wedding chamber set to receive her and her sexagenarian groom. To her great relief, when she said she was tired and wanted to leave, no one stopped her. The minute she got into the door of her apartment, Carlos was on the phone. "They all love you! The phone hasn't stopped ringing!" he said excitedly. She could hear the call waiting feature beeping on his line. "Everyone's crazy about you, baby girl!"

From that night on, Melissa was part of the inner circle. She didn't understand what this Electric Warrior thing was all about; nobody bothered to explain. There were others too—the Lecture Warrior, the Blue Scout, the Orange Scout, The Trackers, The Elements, the Chacmols—most of them attractive younger women. It was a little creepy, all this attention from a man old enough to be her father, but nobody was touching her, nobody was really acting inappropriate—though Carlos had this weird obsession with teaching her to make a fist. Truth be told, the inner circle was kind of fun. She hadn't had a group of friends for many years; it took her mind off her problems, and that was a great relief. The members of the inner circle were all smart and well read. They were up on current events, loved nice clothes and making puns, were always joking around and pulling practical jokes, infantile stuff, like a bucket of water atop a door. They had dinner parties at people's houses and at fancy restaurants; they loved going to Tony Roma's for ribs—in short order, Melissa, formerly a vegetarian, gained ten pounds. Once, at Tracy Kramer's beautiful Craftsman house, Carlos prepared a jelly which he said was made of devil's weed. He said it would make them all fly, but nothing happened to Melissa.

Often, there were madcap performances by something the inner circle called, alternately, the Sorcery Theater or the Theater of Infinity. Written by Bruce Wagner, the skits were hilarious. Slickly produced affairs, complete with props and costumes, most of them were didactic, portraying Carlos's philosophy and his rules, but always in a lampoonist fashion. One favorite skit featured a gypsy fortune teller who picked out members of the audience and proceeded to ruthlessly deconstruct their personalities, their idiosyncrasies, their habits, their oddities—fertile ground, to be sure. Another favorite featured the Chacmols doing nude, martial-arts-like movements with sharp knives in their hands. There was a skit featuring a six-foot dildo; another number was aimed at Melissa and the Lecture Warrior—a musical rendition of "I Don't Know How to Love Him" from *Jesus Christ Superstar*. In time, the Witches—all of whom wore their hair extremely short and dressed in designer clothes—seemed to grow to accept Melissa; they began inviting her along to movies and on shopping trips to Century City Mall, which was walking distance from the Pandora compound.

Toward the end of 1994, Melissa began seeing changes in Carlos, in the inner circle. Though Cleargreen was getting stronger, holding more seminars, the group seemed to become directionless, like they were waiting around, trying to figure out what to do next. Carlos even said as much: "We don't know what to do," he told Melissa, "we don't know where to go, we don't know what's happening." Carlos also started complaining about the tyranny of the Witches. He said they were bossy, that they wouldn't listen to what he said. He spent the whole of one Sunday private class railing about the fact that Taisha had made herself a hamburger one night and refused to make one for him.

He was obviously having trouble seeing—she heard whispers about diabetes—but no one said anything out loud, though everyone had suddenly taken on a new interest in acupuncture and nutrition—an area in which Melissa was very knowledgeable, a fact that seemed to draw the inner circle more closely around her as she began advising them on meal preparation. One thing was certain: Carlos didn't look very well. His skin had become ashen, his hair had turned entirely gray. He wobbled just a bit when he walked. And sometimes, when he came close to talk to her, or to help her practice making a fist, she noticed this peculiar, sour kind of smell about him; it reminded her of the way her mother had smelled before she died.

Then one day Carlos approached her in private. "I'm leaving soon and I'm taking you and everyone else with me," he said.

Melissa was horrified. The first thing that came into her mind was Jim Jones, Kool-Aid, the mass cult suicide in Guyana. She didn't know what to say.

* * *

C.J. Castaneda polished off a tall glass of tap water and turned out the kitchen lights, slowly climbed the stairs to the master bedroom of his rambling, suburban Atlanta house. It was 10:30 p.m. on April 27, 1998, the end of another long and difficult day. The blond, blue-eyed, 36 year old was bone-weary.

A former real estate appraiser and sometime-inventor with a taste for the good life and a near-genius IQ, C.J. had recently started a new business, a chain of drive-up coffee kiosks. The logistics of servicing and running his far-flung mini-enterprise kept him hopping from long before sunup until way past dark, seven days a week. The toll was beginning to show on his handsome countenance; his weight-lifter's build had gone a bit soft around the middle. Sighing, he sat down heavily on his side of the bed, undressed and slipped between the sheets, kissed his wife Lisa goodnight. As was customary, she had settled in with a book, preferring to read for thirty minutes before going to sleep herself. C.J. set his alarm for 4:40, pulled the covers over his head. In moments he was out.

Though few people knew it, Carlton Jeremy Castaneda was Carlos's adopted son, born to Margaret Runyan and a Mormon businessman named Adrian Gerritsen. As with every other chapter in Carlos's life, the story of C.J.'s birth was odd and convoluted.

Six months after Carlos and Margaret were married in Mexico, Carlos had come home to their apartment one afternoon and told her excitedly about meeting an old Indian in a Greyhound bus station near the Arizona border with Mexico. Carlos was enrolled at the time in his first undergraduate anthropology class as UCLA, a course called California Ethnography. His professor had promised an A grade to any student who found an actual Indian informant for a term paper. For months, Carlos had been making trips to the desert, searching for an indigenous wise man to teach him the ancient secrets of hallucinogenic plants. Though he'd once dreamed of becoming a great artist, Carlos now had his sights set on a career as a professor of anthropology. UCLA had a great and competitive department. Surely this desert meeting was an auspicious start on his new path.

Margaret, of course, didn't see things his way at all. She was deeply in love with Carlos; she wanted her husband at home. This was her third marriage, and though it had started out quite romantically—a showdown between two suitors culminating with a midnight road trip to a Mexican justice of the peace—things were already beginning to sour. Besides her suspicion that he was seeing other women, a big stumbling block in their relationship was their respective schedules. While Margaret continued working days as chief operator at the phone company, Carlos was working nights as an accountant in a fancy dress shop in downtown L.A., attending classes during the day. Now, in addition to this hectic schedule, he told Margaret, he was going to start spending his weekends in the desert with this mysterious old man.

Fights and unpleasantness ensued, and soon Carlos moved out of the apartment. Margaret began dating Gerritsen, a tall, handsome Mormon from Utah. Gerritsen was in the clothing business and came frequently to L.A. on buying trips. Finding herself in love with Gerritsen, Margaret asked Carlos for a divorce, and he was surprisingly accommodating. They drove back to Mexico, to the same justice of the peace who had married them. Unbeknownst to Margaret, however, the official didn't actually complete the paperwork for a divorce. Also unbeknownst to Margaret, Gerritsen was an acquaintance of Carlos—it was Carlos who'd actually arranged their first meeting. Furthermore, in a letter filed in connection with a probate case many years later, following Carlos's death, Gerritsen would confirm that Carlos had asked him to father a child with Margaret, a child whom Carlos would then adopt as his own. Margaret and Gerritsen—who was already married to a woman in Salt Lake City—were married in Mexico a short time later. Though the newlyweds never took up housekeeping together, a son was born in August 1961.

Not long after the birth, Carlos came to Margaret and confessed that their Mexican divorce had been a charade, something he'd done to appease her while he did his field work, hoping, he said, that they'd one day reunite as a couple. He explained that they were still married, and that he wanted to adopt her son. As it was, Carlos had been seeing the little tow-headed boy frequently since his birth and had developed a deep attachment. He called the boy Cho-cho; the boy called him Kiki. Carlos took him everywhere—to the beach, to the mountains, to his power spot in Topanga Canyon, to the movies. People got used to seeing the nut brown man carrying the little blond boy everywhere on his shoulders. Often, he brought Cho-cho along to classes at UCLA. When asked, Carlos proudly claimed Cho-cho as his biological son, attributing the obvious differences in coloring to the boy's mother, whom he said was Scandinavian. When Cho-cho was two Carlos appeared at Margaret's apartment with documents from the California Department of Public Health naming Carlos as the natural father of one Carlton Jeremy Castaneda. Her relationship with Gerritsen having long since dissolved, Margaret agreed to sign. A boy needs a father. Carlos was the only one her son had ever known.

Over the next five years, Carlos saw a lot of his Cho-cho; the boy regularly spent nights in his room at Carlos's rented house. In the mornings, for breakfast, Carlos fed him bananas and raw hamburger to help him grow, then walked the boy, hand in hand, to school. In the evenings, while Carlos worked on his book, the two women who would later become the Witches—Florinda Donner-Grau and Carol Tiggs—read Cho-cho his bedtime stories. Before going to sleep, Cho-cho would stand beside Kiki at his desk. "What are you writing?" he'd ask. "I'm writing a book for you, Cho-cho," Carlos would answer. "You're going to make it the most magical of books, because you're the biggest brujo on the planet." Though money was still a problem, Carlos insisted on paying for Cho-cho's tuition at an exclusive Montessori School in Santa Monica—one of his classmates was the daughter of Charlton Heston. Carlos also paid Cho-cho's doctor bills and bought him clothes, sent him for karate and skiing lessons. He would continue paying child support through the mid seventies, when he and Margaret were legally divorced.

When the boy was seven, Margaret and C.J. left L.A., a move that pained Carlos greatly. Carlos continued to correspond with Margaret for many years, writing of his undying love for both her and his Cho-cho, and of his intention to leave any money he might amass to the boy. "I went by your old apt. in the Valley a couple of days ago and got an attack of profound sentimentalism," Carlos wrote to Margaret in August of 1967. "You are my family, dearest Margarita... I owe you a very, very special something. I owe you the most beautiful and magical of all my dreams, my Cho-cho. You brought that dream into my life for one instant, and compared to that instant of dreaming all my other dreams are nothing... Take care! And kiss my Cho-cho's big toe for his Kiki. I keep on telling to myself that I will go hiking with him."

The following year, Carlos dedicated his first book, *The Teachings of Don Juan*, to Cho-cho and Margaret, and he mentioned him in several subsequent books as well, discussing "a little boy that I once knew" with Don Juan, telling him "how my feeling for him would not change with the years or the distance." In 1978, Carlos attend C.J.'s high school graduation in Tempe, Arizona; for the next three years, he paid his college tuition. They were reunited briefly once again a few years later in New York.

Starting in around 1993, however, around the time that Cleargreen and the other companies were formed, Carlos ceased all communications with C.J. and Margaret. Despite his repeated phone calls and letters, C.J. was thwarted in his efforts to contact Carlos by members of Cleargreen, who appeared to be handling all of Carlos's personal business with the outside world. Other friends, including an old roommate and one of Carlos's favorite UCLA professors, were similarly thwarted in their efforts to contact the great man. Frustrated, C.J. heard news of a lecture Carlos was giving in October of 1993, and flew to Santa Monica to try to see him.

C.J. waited in the parking lot outside of the bookstore, and when Carlos spotted the strappingly handsome young man, he seemed overjoyed. He embraced C.J. enthusiastically, kissing him on both cheeks, patting him on the back, speaking with warmth and animation. Their reunion was cut short, however, by two of the Chacmols, who took Carlos one by each arm and hustled him away. As they were moving toward the van to leave, one of the Chacmols retrieved from Carlos a piece of paper with C.J.'s phone number on it, balled it up into a piece of trash.

Three years later, frustrated by Carlos's continuing silence, C.J. paid $400 to attend a Tensegrity workshop where Carlos was slated to appear, once again hoping to reunite with his Kiki. At the door of the workshop, however, he was recognized by the

Cleargreen organizers. They refunded his money and asked him to leave. When he and his wife went across the street to a mall to get something to eat, members of Cleargreen followed at a discreet distance, keeping them under surveillance.

As the 90's progressed, Carlos's contact with old friends ceased altogether. Though he was by now nearly blind, and had to be helped to the stage for lectures, he became increasingly litigious. Lawyers for Cleargreen filed suits attempting to block the publication of writings of a woman named Merilyn Tunneshende, who called herself "The Nagual Woman" and said that she too had studied with Don Juan. In 1995, a suit was initiated by Cleargreen's lawyers against a Toltec teacher and old friend named Victor Sanchez, claiming that the jacket of Sanchez's book about Carlos infringed on Carlos's copyrights. And in 1997, Cleargreen lawyers launched a suit against Margaret Runyan Castaneda and the publishers of her autobiography, *A Magical Journey With Carlos Castaneda*.

In February of 1997, Carlos made his last appearance at a Tensegrity seminar, in Long Beach, California. A spokesman for Toltec Artists said that Carlos had decided "that the seminars were taking their own course and he did not need to be present." Others had a different view of his absence. "He was taking medication, losing weight," said one Carlos watcher, "People were becoming suspicious. If Tensegrity was supposed to lead to health and well-being, why doesn't he look so good?"

In the winter of 1998, Toltec Artists delivered to his publisher the manuscript for Carlos's eleventh book, *The Active Side of Infinity*. In a departure from his other books, *Infinity* takes a somewhat apocalyptic view of the mystical universe, defining it as predatory and populated by shadowy entities called the Flyers, who prey on a man's glowing coat of awareness. Only by practicing Tensegrity, Carlos suggests, can these dark forces be repelled. He also reappraises once again his encounters with Don Juan, concluding strongly that the "total goal" of shamanic knowledge is preparation for facing the "definitive journey—the journey that every human being has to take at the end of his life" to the region that shamans called "the active side of infinity." "We are beings on our way to dying," Don Juan said. "We are not immortal, but we behave as if we were."

Much attention is given in *Infinity* to the departure of the old Nagual, and the notion that an enlightened sorcerer does not die a normal death but is consumed by "the fire from within," a sort of spontaneous combustion, gathering his mortal energy and. carrying the body with him into the next realm. As if preparing his readers for his own leave-taking, Carlos describes in great detail the departure of Don Juan and his party. "I saw then how Don Juan Matus, the Nagual, led the 15 other seers who were his companions ... one by one to disappear into the haze of that mesa, towards the north. I saw how every one of them turned into a blob of luminosity, and together they ascended and floated above the mesa, like phantom lights in the sky. They circled above the mountain once, as Don Juan had said they would do, their last survey, the one for their eyes only, their last look at this marvelous earth, And then they vanished."

Now, fast asleep in the master bedroom of his suburban Atlanta house on the night of April 27, 1998, C.J. Castaneda, once called Cho-cho by the only father he ever knew, became aware of the insistent buzzing of his alarm clock. He opened his eyes, looked at the time: 4:40. As he reached for the snooze button, he happened to notice, sitting in a chair in the corner of the room, glowing a spectral shade of blue, the great man himself, his Kiki, Carlos Castaneda.

Carlos looked young again, and happy, the kind of face he used to make just before he'd lift the young blond boy up up up over his head, onto his shoulders; the kind of face he used to make in the mornings at his rented house, standing over the sink, cutting the little seeds out of the center of a banana because his Cho-cho didn't like that part. Sitting there in the chair, Carlos smiled at C.J. winked one eye. C.J. blinked, blinked again. Carlos was gone.

Seven minutes later, at 4:47, the alarm buzzed again, and C.J. sat up in bed, swung his legs over the side. Shaking off the cobwebs, he rose, padded to the bathroom to take a shower.

Ten minutes later, at 4:57, dressed with wet hair, C.J. took the dog by the collar and left the bedroom, went downstairs, let the dog out the front door, walked to the kitchen, poured some dog food in a bowl. He looked at the clock on the microwave. It said 11:00. He walked over to the kitchen table, picked up his watch. It also said 11:00.

Puzzled, he let the dog back in the front door and returned to the bedroom. The clock by his bed said 11:01.

"Lisa!" he whispered loudly. "Lisa! Wake up!"

His wife stirred, rolled over, looked at the clock. "What do you want?" she asked, "Why are you dressed?"

"How long have you been asleep?" C.J. asked.

"For a while, why?"

"What time?"

"About eleven."

"Lisa, it's 11:01. What do you mean you went to sleep a while ago?"

"What are you talking about!" exclaimed Lisa, growing annoyed.

C.J.'s mind raced. If Lisa had gone to bed at 11:00, how was it that he'd awoken and snoozed and showered and gone downstairs? It was now 11:02. All of that would have had to have taken place in one minute. It was at least twenty minutes worth of activities—she would have still been still reading when he first awoke! The whole thing didn't compute, not at all.

"Why don't you get back in bed?" Lisa suggested, rolling back over, putting her head down on the pillow.

"Holy shit!" said C.J.

"What?"

"I just remembered!"

"What?"

C.J. felt a weird tingling up and down his spine. The hair on the back of his neck stood on end. "I think Carlos is dead."

* * *

The Follower parked his dusty blue Hyundai at the curb in front of Spalding Mortuary, a nondescript brick building in a rundown industrial district just east of Culver City. It was Monday, June 22, 1998, around ten a.m. Though the morning sun was bright, the air was cool; Greg Mamishian was wearing his favorite jacket, a tan corduroy sportscoat with suede elbow patches that once belonged to Carlos. Greg sat silent for a few moments, listening to the engine tick off heat, a short man, fifty years old, with close cropped gray hair and an elfin sparkle in his eyes, girding himself for another mission.

For the past two and a half years, Greg and his wife Gabi had made a hobby of following Carlos. They'd sat outside his compound for hundreds of hours, watching the comings and goings, trying to read between the lines. They'd trailed the Nagual and his party to restaurants and movies, to inner circle practice groups. They'd videotaped him at every opportunity, collected and processed his trash, made what they considered an anthropological study of his life. Along the way, they'd learned much about the great man and the doings of his inner circle, and much about themselves. Every couple needs a binding interest; in an odd, wonderful way, Carlos had become theirs.

It had been more than nine months now since that magical summer night when the fierce Chacmol had caught them red-handed stealing the trash. Though they'd promised the woman from Cleargreen that they were done with their innocent surveillance—thereby avoiding a formal complaint to the police—they'd only lasted about a week before their curiosity and determination had gotten the better of them, and they'd renewed their activities in earnest. Besides changing the time of their trash runs to 3 a.m., things proceeded pretty much as before. The Followers, as Greg had dubbed them, were back in business.

Then, one Sunday afternoon in late February 1998, sitting at their regular post, in a no-parking zone diagonally across the quiet intersection from Carlos's low-slung compound, the Followers saw a car pull up to the Pandora Avenue gate, a blue Ford Crown Victoria that belonged to one of the Chacmols. As it slowed to a stop, several members of the inner circle came quickly out of the house, moved toward the back door of the car. Riveted, Greg and Gabi watched in disbelief as they ministered to the great man, helping him gingerly out of the back seat, hauling him to his feet. For some time it had been obvious that Carlos's vision had been failing; they'd found insulin syringes and prescription medicine bottles in the trash. Now it was clear that his health had taken a dramatic turn for the worse. Carlos was thin and fragile, floppy like a rag doll. His skin was grayish green, his hair was very short, there were dark circles around his eyes; he had the skeletal appearance of an internee in a concentration camp. He didn't so much walk as shuffle, supported on either side by Chacmols, steadied from behind by the Blue Scout.

Gabi looked at Greg, Greg looked at Gabi. A wave of extreme sadness washed over them. There was no mistaking the fact that Carlos was dying, that their marvelous folly would soon be coming to an end. At the edge of the sadness was something else, a sort of bitter aftertaste of disappointment: If Carlos was planning, as he'd promised, to leave the Earth in full awareness with his boots on, in a flash of light for the Second Attention like Don Juan, he had better hurry. From the looks of him, he didn't have much time.

Over the next weeks and months, the Followers saw no more of Carlos. His public appearances at seminars and workshops ended; the private classes at the dance studio came to a halt; he never again went out for a movie or a meal. Meanwhile, the level of activity at the compound increased dramatically. People came and went in shifts several times a day, bringing with them medical supplies and covered dishes of food. The members of the inner circle all got new cars, mostly mid-sized Fords. A new roof was put on the house, many other small repairs were made as well; the Followers got the feeling that the place was being readied for sale. When landscapers arrived and began tearing up the internal courtyard of the compound, the Followers wondered if they were digging a grave. Then one evening they observed Taisha Abelar packing her van with stacks of files and documents and a big cooler full of supplies. She was in an obvious hurry. The Followers wondered: Were they taking Carlos to Mexico to die? In mid-April, Gabi and Greg observed what seemed to be a flurry of packing and cleaning and organizing. Their trash take that week was unbelievably fruitful: clothes, statues and knicknacks, flatware, curtains, supplies—there were 16 bags, more than twice the normal amount. Once upon a time they'd have been overjoyed by such fabulous gleanings. Now they felt only curiosity and sorrow.

During the week of April 22, Greg and Gabi left off their surveillance in favor of a rare, seven-day vacation to Kauai, the honeymoon they hadn't yet gotten around to taking. When they returned, tanned and rested, the first thing they did was drive to Carlos's compound.

The place was empty. There was no one there. No cars, no people, no furniture inside. The only thing in the trash can was some construction debris and a few fast food wrappers. Several trips over the next few days confirmed their suspicions: The Sorcerer and his party had disappeared.

For the next six weeks, things at the compound remained unchanged. Meanwhile, phone lines and Internet chat rooms were buzzing with speculation. There were rumors that Carlos and his party had bought a big luxury yacht and had embarked on a world cruise. Others said that the inner circle had taken Carlos to Mexico to "leave." Still others posited that Carlos had died and the Witches had committed suicide in solidarity. Everyone associated, it seemed, had an opinion. Cleargreen remained suspiciously mum, continuing to schedule new seminars, carrying on business as usual.

Then, in mid June, C.J. Castaneda received a notice from the probate court in Los Angeles. On April 27, 1998, the letter informed him, Carlos Castaneda had died. Though C.J. and Margaret were mentioned in the will, they were left nothing of the estate, which some estimated to be worth as much as $20 million. In the six-page document, which was signed and dated April 23, Carlos explicitly distanced himself from his Cho-cho, stating in Article 1 that "although I once treated him as if he were my son, C.J. Castaneda is not my son, natural or adopted." All monies and property and future rights to his work were bequeathed to something called The Eagle's Trust, the officers of which were members of Carlos's inner circle, men and women who also served as the officers of Cleargreen, Toltec Artists and the other corporations. Outraged that Cleargreen had failed to exercise common decency and notify him of his Kiki's death, hurt that he'd been disavowed and disinherited by the only father he had ever known, C.J. called the *Los Angeles Times* and tipped them off to the death. Later, he would initiate a suit against Cleargreen and Carlos's executors, claiming that the will was a fraud. After nine months of legal wrangling, C.J. would drop the suit.

The story ran on the front page of the *Times* on Friday, June 19. "Carlos Castaneda... apparently died two months ago in the same way that he lived: quietly, secretly, mysteriously?"

According to his death certificate, the *Times* story said, Carlos had died of liver cancer on April 27, at the age of 72. In typical Carlos fashion, the death certificate listed his occupation as "teacher," and his employer as the Beverly Hills School District, for which he'd never worked. It also said that he had never been married. Immediately following the death, it was reported, his body had been cremated, his ashes spirited away to Mexico. Explaining why no one was notified about his passing, Carlos's long-time lawyer, Debra Drooze, was quoted as saying: "He didn't like attention. He always made sure people did not take his picture or record his voice. He didn't like the spotlight. Knowing that, I didn't take it upon myself to issue a press release."

The next day, on their website, Cleargreen issued a statement to the faithful. Their position was a bit different than the lawyer's. "Carlos Castaneda left the world the same way that his teacher, Don Juan Matus did: with full awareness," the statement read in part. "The cognition of our world of everyday life does not provide for a description of a phenomenon such as this. So in keeping with the terms of legalities and record keeping that the world of everyday life requires, Carlos Castaneda was declared to have died."

Having read both the article in the *Times* and the posting on the Web, Greg and Gabi, like many others, didn't know what to think. So many odd and wonderful things had happened in connection with Carlos, so many mystical events and occurrences that seemed to have no explanation in the world of ordinary reality. Now they wanted to know how the story ended. They needed to know the truth. Had he died like a man? Had he left like a sorcerer? Which was it? For so many years now, Gabi and Greg and countless others around the world had set their reality compass by the teachings of Carlos and Don Juan. There was a need for some kind of closure. It didn't help any that all the Witches had disappeared. When asked, Cleargreen would only say that the Witches were "traveling."

Using the detective skills he'd honed to a sharp edge over the last several years, Greg tracked down Carlos's death certificate. A little leg work revealed that Carlos's body had not been taken to the mortuary that was specified, but to a different place, one with an unlisted telephone number called the Spalding Mortuary.

And so it was, on the Monday morning following the announcement of Carlos's death in the *L.A. Times*, that Greg got out of his car and walked through the unlocked door of a nondescript brick building in a run-down industrial district just east of Culver City. He was going to get to the bottom of this mystery, once and for all.

He was met in the hallway by a tall, elderly black gentleman, who kindly asked his business. Standing there in the dark hallway, wearing the corduroy sportscoat that had once belonged to Carlos himself, Greg explained that Spalding Mortuary had recently cremated the remains of a man named Carlos Castaneda. This man, Greg continued, had claimed to be a great and powerful sorcerer and had followers all over the world. Though his teachings were many, Greg explained, first among them was the notion that an enlightened sorcerer does not die a normal death, but rather is consumed by something called "the fire from within," a sort of spontaneous combustion, wherein he gathers his mortal energy and leaves for the next realm, taking his body with him.

"I am here to find out the truth," Greg told the elderly gentleman in his typically earnest but ironic style. "What I want to know is this: Did he burn with the fire from within? Or did you burn him?"

The gentleman regarded Greg for several long moments—trying, no doubt, to decide what to do. Greg seemed harmless enough. He was polite and appeared sane. He was obviously deeply aggrieved. But what Greg was saying, well—he'd seen and heard many things in his years in the mortuary business, but this took it all: he'd never heard anything so ridiculous in his life. "Please sit down," he said at last.

After ten minutes or so, a well-dressed, older woman appeared before Greg and asked him to repeat his business. She listened intently, nodding her head, wearing a sympathetic face. Until, that is, he got to the part about "the fire from within." She reared back her head and laughed out loud.

Greg looked at the woman and smiled. He raised his hands, palms up, shrugged his shoulders. She was a tall, heavyset, regal woman, the model of a family matriarch. She leaned down and put her arms around Greg, gave him a tender, motherly hug. "He has gone to a better place," she said, patting his back.

Greg stepped back from her embrace. "I know that," he said, regarding her quizzically. "But what I want to know is: which better place. Are you sure you cremated him?"

"I watched it myself," she said confidently.

"You're positive?"

"His spirit is gone, baby."

Greg thanked the woman, turned and went outside, to his car. He opened the door, started to get in, then stopped himself. He felt numb, an odd mixture of disappointment and relief. For what must have been the one millionth time over the six years, the words of scholar Richard DeMille floated through his mind. *Castaneda wasn't a common con man, he lied to bring us the truth. His stories are packed with truth, though they are not true stories, which he said they are... This is a sham-man bearing gifts, an ambiguous spellbinder dealing simultaneously in contrary commodities—wisdom and deception.*

Greg removed his favorite jacket, the tan corduroy sportscoat with suede elbow patches that once belonged to Carlos, and threw it unceremoniously into the back seat of the car. It was time to move on.

Death in Venice

Lil' Sleeper and Margarita are hanging out at Yogi's, all three sitting on his bed. The room is dark, narrow, smoky. A towel is jammed against the bottom of the door.

"I forgot to tell you," Yogi says. "Sleeper called."

"Yeah?" asks Lil' Sleeper.

"He asked what have we done to pay back Culver City."

"Pay 'em back for what?"

"You know, man. The drive-by at the park. Those *vatos* who shot at us. Remember, *ese?*"

Lil' Sleeper chews his thumb and thinks for a minute. The TV flickers, the radio plays rap, a table fan moves air back and forth. He turns to Margarita, his girlfriend. "When this happen?"

Margarita's eyes pan slowly toward his face. They've been dating for a year. She is wearing a black miniskirt and a necklace of hickeys, a pair of three-inch heels she bought two weeks ago on her fourteenth birthday. Her hair is shoulder length, crowned at the front with a stiff pompadour—a four-inch tiara of bangs combed skyward and encased in Aqua Net hairspray. She blinks. She shrugs. She don't remember, either. One day be like the next.

Lil' Sleeper chews his thumb some more. The skin at the tip, just below the nail, is burned and crusty, a condition the homeboys call Bic Thumb. Like Yogi, he is nineteen. He is wearing a nylon sweat suit and high-top Adidas. His hair is black as tar, clipped short and oiled straight back from a widow's peak. His lashes are long and curly, his eyes are bloodshot, one of his front teeth is missing. The first time he was arrested he was six years old; he stole a TV from his grammar school. Last year, he was arrested eleven times for being under the influence of heroin and two times for being under the influence of PCP, a drug he likes because "when you do it, it be hard for you to walk and think."

As days in the neighborhood go, this one started off pretty well. At 10:00 this morning, Lil' Sleeper and Margarita ran into a crack dealer they know. He kicked down some love, gave them some free drugs, the dregs of last nights stash—a couple of five- and ten-dollar rocks and a bunch of crumbs. The pair went immediately to Yogi's place and smoked it all in fifteen minutes. Now they need more.

Sitting on the edge of the bed, Lil' Sleeper is a ramrod. His mouth is pulled back in a tight grimace. Above his lip, among the faint stirrings of a mustache, are little drops of sweat. His teeth are clenched; you can see the strain in the muscles of his jaw and in the cords of his neck, upon which is tattooed, in big blue letters, the logo of his gang, V-13.

He plucks an ice cube from his glass, holds it up, regards it in the light. "Wouldn't you like a rock this size?" He sounds like a kid wishing for a pony for his birthday—which in fact he did when he was ten.

"*Yea-ah!*" Yogi enthuses.

"How big would you say this was, a fifty?" Lil' Sleeper asks.

"A righteous five-oh," Yogi opines.

Lil' Sleeper loses himself in his daydream; hope pops like a flashbulb in his eyes, and then the light recedes. His attention drifts to the carpet. There are lots of little white pieces of paper and lint and cloth and cigarette ash down there. To him, each piece looks like a rock. Could be a rock. He has an urge to reach down with his index finger and feel around for *pedasos,* little pieces of crack cocaine. That he *knows* there are no *pedasos* on the carpet, that he's way too methodical to have dropped anything, doesn't matter at all, because something strong makes him want to get down on his hands and knees on the filthy rug in the dark, musky, narrow room and touch each little piece of paper and lint and cloth and ash and test its composition. There are no crumbs. He knows that. It doesn't matter. A few minutes ago, he tried to smoke a sesame seed. It tasted like burnt toast when he fired it up in his pipe, which is really a piece of broken-off car antenna stuffed with Choir-boy brand copper scouring sponge—the kind without the soap. A recent letter in a local weekly paper complained about the recent epidemic of broken car antennas. Now you know.

"So what are we going to do about Culver City?" Yogi asks. "Sleeper say that if we down for the neighborhood, we gotta pay them back."

Lil' Sleeper looks up from the floor. He and Yogi are members of the Venice Gang, among the oldest and most proud of the 400 gangs in Los Angeles. For more than thirty years, Chicano homeboys have claimed this neighborhood, one square mile of palm trees and poverty in the middle of Venice, California, a little piece of ghetto encrusted in the heart of the California lifestyle like plaque in an artery—long established, nearly impossible to dislodge. Ten years ago, when Yogi and Lil' Sleeper were still playing with toys, war was raging in the neighborhood; V-13 was locked in epic battles with all the gangs that surrounded it—Santa Monica, Culver City, the Shoreline Crips, the black gang with whom they share Oakwood, the official name for the section of Venice in which they live. At the time, the *Los Angeles Times* devoted a special section to the unrest. "DEATH, DAILY VIOLENCE BECOME WAY OF LIFE FOR NEIGHBORHOOD," said the lead headline, one of twelve screamers in the twelve-page pullout. The Los Angeles police department's now-infamous CRASH unit (Community Resources Against Street Hoodlums) cut its teeth in Venice; the National Guard walked the streets for a period, too. A whole generation of Venice homeboys went to jail, became addicted to heroin, or died.

These days, Venice still gets its CRASH sweeps: low-key Tuesday and Thursday night affairs. The *pop pop pop* of automatic-weapons fire is still part of the everyday soundtrack of squealing tires, cursing homeboys, laughing children, and thumping rap. But aside from Popo—a homeboy who lost his cool during a burglary and slit the throat of L.A. city councilwoman Ruth Galanter—Venice hasn't been in the news at all lately. South-central Los Angeles is where the action is now. There, black gangs have adopted the gangsta lifestyle pioneered by the Mexican *cholos* of yore; they have begun a reign of entrepreneurial terror that has turned the L.A. gang culture inside out. For generations, the poor and the powerless of Southern California—as in every urban center across the world—banded together to form neighborhood self-protection societies. They fought for the safety of their streets and for some measure of self-respect. Back in the day, in Los Angeles, the Chicanos were ascendant. Gangs like V-13 were strong and proud.

Today, gangs are no longer about turf and respect. Instead, they are about drugs and money. Crack has done to V-13 what the police and the National Guard and other gangs have been trying to do for years.

Now, in Yogi's room, Lil' Sleeper grinds his teeth some more. He looks beseechingly at his homie: "You think you can get twenty bucks from your moms?"

"*My* moms?" asks Yogi. "What about yours?"

"I asked her yesterday, *ese*."

They both look at Margarita.

* * *

The drive-by happened two nights ago.

Yogi, Lil' Sleeper, and Margarita were there, and so were Wormy, Linda, and a couple more *vatos* and *heinas*, dudes and chicks. They were kickin' it on a grassy field behind Broadway Elementary, hunkered in the middle of their own neighborhood, their home turf. Someone had brought a couple *pistos*, big bottles of Colt 45 malt liquor. Someone had some *yeska*, Mexican marijuana, ditch weed. Four of the homies were *shermed*, high on *frios*, which are menthol cigarettes dipped in a bottle of liquid

PCP—two of them were crawling around on all fours, unable to walk. Yogi, Lil' Sleeper, Panther, and a white guy named Mike, your reporter, were taking turns crouching behind a wall, doing blasts, taking hits of crack.

Right around midnight, Wormy was smoking another *frio.* Loud and grandiose, he was telling everyone about the time in jail he was stabbed in the head. After that, he began talking about his father, a white man who had abandoned his mom. When the *frio* was finished, he got very quiet. His face assumed a strange, tortured expression.

And then he went *off.*

He smashed a bottle on the sidewalk, uttered incantations to the devil, danced around in the grass. He locked his focus on the white guy, stood over me and shook his fists. "Prejudice!" he bellowed, over and over. I tried to remain calm and still. At last, Yogi and Lil' Sleeper tackled him. No matter how fucked up they were, during the six weeks I was with them, my boys always had my back.

After a few minutes, things got mellow again. Everybody was chillin', smokin' out, drinkin', having a laugh.

And then, out of the darkness came a souped-up, '65 Chevy, white on blue with mag wheels. It squealed around the corner. Shots rang out: quick loud pops from a semi-automatic. From the sound of it, a .22-caliber.

The rounds sizzled the air above our heads. Small bullets can do a lot of damage; they get inside your body and ping around, tearing up organs. Yogi rolled on top of Linda. Margarita rolled on top of Lil' Sleeper. Everyone else hit the dirt.

And then it was over. A single tail light receded from their territory. In the nighttime stillness, you could hear hoots of laughter coming from the car.

"There go those motherfuckers from Culver City," somebody said.

"Cheese eaters!" Yogi yelled.

"*Putos*!"

Margarita pointed in the opposite direction across the field.

It was Sleeper. He did not look pleased.

Twenty-seven years old, Sleeper is an OG, an original gangsta, one of the leaders in the 'hood. There are no elected officials in V-13; in a gang, a leader makes himself. Rank is bestowed naturally, over the course of time, by dint of service, reputation, and personality. Sleeper has a thick scar across his cheek, two bullet holes in his side, another in his shoulder. To this day, he carries a shotgun pellet in his penis. He calls it his Mexican tickler. "What the fuck was that?" he screamed at his young homies.

"Just some of those cheese eaters from Culver City," Yogi said matter-of-factly.

"*Those* motherfuckers? Again?"

Nobody said a word. The two who had earlier been nonambulatory were now passed out on the grass.

Sleeper shook his head sadly. Lately, he thinks, everything is fucked up in the neighborhood. Everything has changed. These younger homeboys know as well as he does that if someone disrespects you—if he calls you a name, if he mad-dogs you, if he owes you money, if he shoots at you, if he talks shit about your old lady, if he makes you angry about anything at all—there is only one thing you're supposed to do. You go get your gun out of its hiding place, you hunt him down, you cap him, you bust a grape. Or, if you can't find *him*, you cap one of his homeboys. You don't drive by—that's for cheese eaters, something else new in the picture. For years the homies from Venice and Culver City have been shooting each other, but it was always done face to face. That was always the rule. Yes, there were rules. A code of honor if you will: You don't shoot from a car. You don't shoot at a house. You don't do things to jeopardize innocent children or family members. A few years ago, one of the Venice homeboys took a shot at a rival gang member who was standing outside a church. A mother and her child were killed. As soon as they heard what happened, the Venice homeboys beat up their own *vato*. He was banished from the neighborhood.

Sleeper looked off in the direction the Chevy had retreated. He hocked a fat lugie on the ground. "Somebody better do something soon—or *all* y'all gonna have to deal with *me*."

* * *

Since 1900, when "Venice of America" was built, complete with canals, as a sort of residential theme park by the Pacific Ocean, the Oakwood section, just adjacent, has been poor and predominantly nonwhite, a little patch of blight along the pricey Southern California coast. The older families date back four or five generations, though the notion of generations can be deceptive here. Many of the women become pregnant at fifteen or sixteen; thirty year old grandmothers are not difficult to find.

The neighborhood claimed by V-13 is a ramshackle collection of bungalows with front and back yards. Invariably, there will be one or more older-model Chevrolets around the properties, in various states of repair, and maybe an old stove in the back yard. Women who work outside the neighborhood tend to drive small Japanese imports. The walls of all the buildings and fences are covered with graffiti, riotous scrawlings that identify the gang and its members by their street names—each gang and each man has, in effect, his own logo.

Inside, the houses are tidy and clean; the furnishings and knickknacks are inexpensive but lovingly kept. Wedding, graduation, and post-boot camp military portraits of family members are displayed high on the walls, above the typical sightline, lending the pictures an iconic air. The television burns twenty-four/seven; the electronic hearth is always on. Typically, there is a large living room with lots of sofas and chairs. The seating is plush and comfortable—in general, the dwellers are a substantial lot, owing to a diet heavy with lard and tortillas and sweets; in the eat-in kitchen, there is always an iron skillet of beans on the stove, fresh tortillas on the table. Every other room, including the back porch, is used as a bedroom. People will also sleep at night in the living room.

Typically, four or five generations of relatives live in one house. Great-grandma shares a bedroom with auntie. Grandma and an orphaned great-niece will share another. A high-ranking daughter—often the one with the best job—will have a room to herself. A young couple will also have a room. If they have a small child, the child will sleep with the ranking female. The females of the clan share an elaborate network of responsibilities. Everyone cooks, cleans, and takes care of the kids. Young couples have the fewest responsibilities. They are encouraged to sleep late, to make more babies. The older children take care of the younger children. They grow up taking care of one another. One sixteen-year-old mother, when told about the notion of "unwed motherhood" knit her brows in puzzlement. "I been taking care of babies since I was five or six," she giggled. "I love babies. I don't see it as a *bad* thing."

The women run the household with a loving but firm hand. Grandma or Great-grandma holds the lease; all the women work in some fashion or another, some off the books so they can still collect from the government. Because the homeboys live at the pleasure of their wives' or girlfriends' mother or grandmother, and because many have no job and no prospects, they are low in the family pecking order—treated not so differently from the children. Not much is expected of them, either.

Until recently, the word *gang* wasn't used in connection with V-13. Gang was something the police called them, something the newspapers called them. To themselves, they were, and have always been, simply a *neighborhood*: people who live in a place where they've lived all their lives, where their parents have lived all *their* lives. To the Chicanos of Oakwood, this one square mile is their village, their home, their world, a society within society. Everyone knows everyone, and they have known each other since they were born. When somebody disrespects the neighborhood—when somebody from Culver City hits Lutie's mom on the head with a bumper jack, or takes a knife to Beaver, or a bat to Tavo, or shoots Gato in the back—the neighborhood is supposed to make sure that somebody from Culver City is bumper-jacked or knifed or clubbed or shot. It is the job of the men to protect the honor of the neighborhood. This is the meaning of the expression "down for the 'hood." Either you is or you ain't.

Lately the youngbloods of V-13 have been eatin' cheese. Three times over the past ten days, gang members from Culver City, Chicanos from the projects in the town next door to Venice, have driven through the neighborhood and taken potshots at Venice people. Unfortunately, Yogi and Lil' Sleeper and the rest have been too fucked up on crack to continue their four-generation cycle of violence. Even the social workers have begun to notice.

"I remember the Venice from when I was gang banging," says Marianne Diaz, 29, a former member of the Compadres, another Chicano gang in Los Angeles. She is now an outreach worker with Community Youth Gang Services.

"Venice is such a big, old gang," she says. "Even back in the day they had, like, maybe a thousand homeboys. They were down. People respected them. Venice, Lennox, South Los, and Eighteenth Street. Those were your four big gangs. Everyone has heard of Venice. I mean, if you got busted, you were gonna see twenty or thirty of them down in the pen, and they were the ones running things. Just about every older Venice homeboy I meet is a *veterano*," an ex-con.

In Venice, she says, a high percentage of the males over fifteen have been to jail or to juvenile. "He figures the system is against him, that no one wants to give him a chance. And he also figures there's a good chance he will die tomorrow. It is a very live-for-today society." In his nineteen years, Lil' Sleeper has done a total of four years behind bars; Yogi is about to go off and serve a one-year sentence. He says he's innocent of the actual crime for which he was found guilty, but he's taking it like a man: "I figured I'd already done about thirty or forty *other* burglaries. They had to get me for one of them."

Being respected in the neighborhood for being an ex-con is only one aspect of a curious system of beliefs in Venice. Take the Gonzales family. On a typical Saturday night in the living room there is popcorn and a video, adults and kids. Three people in the room, of varying ages, are nodding out from heroin. A joint of *yeska* is being passed around. The daughter's boyfriend and two of his friends are bustling in and out from the back yard, smoking crack. At one point, Great-grandma looks up from the movie. "Oh, Thumper, I *know* you are doing that shit again." She laughs heartily, setting her chins jiggling. "You are sprunger than a motherfucker!" Everybody in the room guffaws.

Over the years, one homeboy's father, a $22,000-a-year city employee, has borrowed a total of $40,000 to bail out and defend his son for various crimes. Another's father took a week off from work to help his son kick his heroin habit. "I just love my boy," the father says. "What would you do?"

By the time gang members reach the age of twenty-five—if they live that long—they usually move toward a more settled life. Many work in city sanitation and maintenance. Delivery services are another good shot for ex-cons. Almost all of them have children; their culture puts a high value on the young; they want to see their *niños* grow up. War is a young man's game. The OGs rest on their laurels.

"The older homeboys are saying that the younger guys, all they care about is getting high," says Diaz. "They're telling them, 'You like to wear Venice on your hat, you like to write your name on the walls and throw up a hand sign and get tattoos all over your body, but you won't bust a grape on nobody.' "

Back in the 1940s and 1950s, says Diaz, the Chicano gangs that emerged in Southern California were "more or less derived from the Hispanic culture." Descendants of the Mexican *banditos*, and later of the zoot suiters, they inherited a macho culture dedicated to the preservation of territory and respect.

"Now," says Diaz, "things are changing. The rock cocaine has come in, and the blacks have taken over the gang thing. My partner, who is black, he always tells me, 'My people took your idea of gangs and totally bent it and turned it around and took away any of the pride or the respect.' I think that's true. It's like before, in the old days, the leader of a gang was the homeboy who was downest. Now it's the homeboy who is richest. In Venice, nobody's got nothing anymore. It's all about getting high."

* * *

Lil' Sleeper and Yogi are back in the room, both of them sitting on the bed. It's morning. Or maybe it's afternoon. They've been smoking a few rocks.

"Psssss t. Psssssssst!"

Yogi starts. His eyes go wide. "What was that?" he whispers.

"Wha?" asks Lil' Sleeper. He looks up from the carpet, where he's been searching for crumbs.

"That noise," Yogi says. He turns down the radio, switches off the fan, cocks an ear.

"What noise?" Lil' Sleeper repeats.

"Hey, *Yogi*! Lemme in, *ese*!"

Yogi pulls back the curtain on the window over his bed. Outside there is daylight. The palms rustle in the breeze. Into the room waft the scents of salty sea, pink hydrangeas, refried beans, blue exhaust from souped-up cars. It is Panther. He holds up a dove, a twenty-dollar rock, about the size of a marble.

Yogi's bedroom is the unofficial clubhouse for the members of the Little Banditos, a twelve-member *cliqua* within the V-13 gang, which numbers roughly 300. A *cliqua* is an age-affinity group of homies who were all jumped into the gang at the same time—sort of like a pledge class in a fraternity. Like a soccer or basketball club, the Venice gang has a number of *cliquas* for different age groups, ranging from early teens to late twenties. There are the Banditos, the Little Banditos, the Tiny Banditos, the Midget Banditos. Likewise, within the gang, there are *cliquas* of Locos, Winos, Chucos, and Dukes, all of them with subgroups ranging from Midgets to Bigs.

Whenever the Little Banditos come by Yogi's crib, they follow the same procedure. They check first with Yogi at the window, then they go around to the front of the house and knock politely at the door. Permitted entrance, they exchange pleasantries in the front room—like so many brown-skinned Eddie Haskels, talkin' polite shit to Yogi's mom, his grandfather, and his little sister. Then they walk down the hallway to the back room, Yogi's crib. His mom thinks they're watching television and videos all day long. Or maybe she doesn't. Over the past month, since he got his tax-refund check (he worked for his uncle's landscaping company last summer), Yogi has not been away from his room for longer than an hour. The more crack you do, the harder it is to leave the pipe and sally forth.

"First hit!" Yogi calls, in the same manner he calls "shotgun" if you're driving him somewhere.

"It's *my* rock," Panther protests.

"Yeah, but it's my *room.*" There is nothing worse than having a rock and nowhere to smoke it. You need somewhere cool and quiet. Somewhere nobody will bother you. If you don't pay attention, you can fuck off your high, which means you don't take advantage of the rush. It's only there for a little while. You can easily miss it. And then, all you're left with is the jittery need for more.

Panther hands over the rock. Yogi slices it with a razor blade, puts a piece the size of a small aquarium stone into his car-antenna-pipe. He melts it some with a Bic lighter, blows out all the air in his lungs, takes a blast. You can't hit it too hard or the hit will liquefy and you'll lose it; later you'll have to scrape it out of the pipe. The resin is like the mint after dessert. As soon as Yogi finishes his hit, Lil' Sleeper snatches the pipe from his hand; he and Panther begin to argue over who's next. Yogi sits back and closes his eyes. Finally he exhales—a light, clean smoke that smells of ether. Upon his next intake of fresh air, there is a supercharge effect—an instant explosion of pleasure inside his head, an orgasmic body rush. It drills a hole from the top of his scalp down to his groin, and then it drills another between his ears—an ecstatic, physical, electric sign of the cross. The music from the radio comes flooding into his head. His brain buzzes. He smiles cherubically, slightly crosseyed.

Then the smile recedes, the feeling starts to fade, like the light when you turn off the TV, the long white line that dissolves into a dot, then disappears. He begins thinking about the next hit.

One more hit. That's *all* he can think about, all he cares about. His teeth are clenched, his jaw muscles stand, his throat tightens. Everything inside tightens. His veins constrict, his dick shrivels, his heart pounds. He lights another cigarette.

With each subsequent hit, the rush is less intense, but the desire is *more* intense. With heroin, you have a twice-a-day obligation. You fix morning and night and forget about it. Crack is moment to moment. You do a hit, feel the rush, start obsessing immediately about the next hit. About getting more. More. One more hit. If you could stop thinking about it for thirty minutes, the urge would pass. You'd be jittery and speedy, but you could ride it out. But you can't *not* think about it. Your every thought is focused on the next hit.

But the next hit is never as good.

You don't care. You keep going.

You are *sprung*.

* * *

"So what are we gonna do?" Yogi asks. He is sitting on the bed in his narrow room. It is noon on another day. The drugs are gone, again. Lil' Sleeper is here, as usual. Panther is out trying to get some money some *vato* owes him.

"Let's go get a rock," Lil' Sleeper says, as if it's a new idea.

"You got any *fedia*?"

"No."

"You do *so.*"

"I do not."

"Don't bullshit me, *ese.*"

The way you find rock in the neighborhood is this: You walk outside of your house.

Day or night, rock is always for sale. You can buy it from men or women, boys or girls. You can buy it on corners, in alleys, though windows, inside apartment buildings. The dealers here don't even bother with packaging—no glassine envelopes, no vials. They sell the *pedasos* loose. The rocks are hard, white, crystalline, irregular. Cooked down from powder cocaine, using baking soda to trigger the chemical changes, they are pure and insoluble. The dealers stash the *pedasos* in their socks, in baggies, in pockets, beneath their tongues—a place the cops haven't yet learned to look; it won't be long. In the coming years, to frustrate the chain-of-custody considerations of the law, a more elaborate sales system will have to be developed: one guy to take the money, one guy to monitor a stash that nobody physically possesses, an underage kid to deliver the actual rock. For now, though, things are simple. The dealer has the rocks. He works the curb. He *slings*.

There is constant commerce. There are businesslike slickers with theme raps ("I'm Billy D./Stick with me"). There are hot babes, cold gangstas, skinny rock dawgs—by five in the morning, they are scrapping and arguing like extras from the set of *Night of the Living Dead*, trying to sell another rock to go score more. Besides the members of V-13 and their families—one night I partied with a group of women in their thirties and forties, all of whom were gainfully employed; they smoked *way* more crack than the homies could ever even afford—the customers are a steady stream of *gavachos*, white people in nice cars, residents of nearby Marina Del Ray, Santa Monica, and Beverly Hills. The dealers rush aggressively into the street, surrounding the cars, sticking their hands inside, jockeying and fending for position... vibrating, clenching, exhorting, "Take mine!" "Me!" "I got you!"

Most of the dealers are *miatas*, derogatory Chicano slang for African-American—in this case members of the Shoreline Crips, whose families have coexisted with the Chicanos in Oakwood for years. Lately, there has been peace between the two gangs. The Shorelines have no beef with the *vatos* smoking up all the product they can sell.

Sleeper remembers the days when things were different. "Nineteen seventy-seven was the first I remember somebody getting killed that I actually knew," he says. "And then, *bang*, all of a sudden there were like ten shootings a week. Homies were dropping left and right on both sides. It was all-out war. When we walked down the street, we carried a gun. We wore the whole outfit, the khakis and the Pendletons, the hairnets, the bandannas, the hats, the overcoats, the whole bit. We was clean, five creases in every shirt, and we ironed them ourselves. Between me, my brother and my father, we used to go through two cans of spray starch a week.

"I sometimes carried a twelve-gauge shotgun under my overcoat. It was like the Wild West, man. You'd have homeboys on the roof, homeboys behind the trees, guns everywhere. For a while, when the National Guard had the streets barricaded, you could only get in by police escort. If a house got burned, the fire department wouldn't go in until sunrise. It was up to you to put it out. We was down, homeboy, wasn't nobody meaner."

In 1979, the media discovered the gang problem by the sea. The *Los Angeles Times* published their special report—an entire section. There were stories of stray bullets, innocent victims, grieving mothers, shattered lives, midnight death.

"THE TROUBLE IN OAKWOOD," read a subhead on the front page. "Swept by smog-free ocean breezes, bordered on the south by the affluent playground called Marina del Rey," the text read, "Oakwood is a strangely incongruous center of poverty and tragedy. While crime and gang violence tear at the community from within, mounting coastal real-estate values threaten to crush it from without."

At that time, the drugs of choice in the neighborhood were *chiva* and PCP. *Chiva* is Mexican slang for "goat." In this case, it's also slang for black tar heroin imported from Mexico When *chiva* was the thing, the Chicanos ruled the L.A. drug trade. They had the cars and the money and the guns. They sold the heroin to the *miatas* and reaped the profits.

Since crack came to the 'hood, the *miatas* have been in control. The struggle to stay high is a difficult job. The homeboys beg their mothers or their wives or girlfriends for five or ten dollars. They say they have to get a new driver's license, or they find some other official-sounding excuse. They say they need a new asthma inhaler or another small, expensive thing that they can rip off from a drug store and produce later to back up their story. Scam done, they buy a couple hits and smoke. Then they start all over again, scamming to get more. Many have sold their tools and their father's tools. There are amazing deals floating around Venice at three in the morning—whole automotive tune-up kits for under fifty dollars, VCRs for twenty-five. Many in Venice have also sold their guns, which is probably another reason the Venice homeboys have been unable to muster the manpower to pay back Culver City. Lil' Sleeper, for one, sold his shotgun about a month ago. One night, someone offered me a .22-caliber semiautomatic Ruger rifle for the price of a twenty-dollar rock. Absent something of value to sell, the homeboys will do a robbery or burglary, though when you're sprung, that sort of business takes way too long. And then there's the business of fencing the goods—gratification too long delayed.

"The worst thing," says Joe Alarcon, a former Lennox gang member who now works for Youth Gang Services, "is that at this point we don't have much to offer Venice. The problems are even bigger in South Central. Down there we're getting, like, five homicides a week. The black areas are really bad. On a daily basis, something like 85 to 90 percent of all crimes in Los Angles are being committed by Bloods and Crips. Those guys are crazy; they just don't care. Because our resources are limited, we've had to concentrate on the areas that are the worst. We've kind of let Venice fall through the cracks, I'm afraid."

* * *

Another day in Yogi's room. Yogi, Lil' Sleeper, and Margarita are on the bed.

Lil' Sleeper:

"How much *fedia* you got?"

Yogi:

"Two dollars, homes."

"I got two, too," says Lil' Sleeper. Really, he has five. He turns to Margarita. "You got *fedia*?"

Margaritas eyes are large, brown, empty. She looks like a beautiful, underage zombie model. One at a time, she works three crumpled dollar bills out of the front pocket of her super-tight denim mini-skirt. Finished at last, she holds the bills aloft like a prize.

"That's six," Lil' Sleeper announces. He snatches the bills from her hand.

"Seven," Yogi contradicts.

"Wha'?"

"Two and two plus three equals *seven*."

And then: A series of hard knocks on the door—*bang bang bang*.

Everybody ramrods. Eyes like saucers. *What the fuck, ese*?

Yogi turns down the radio and the fan. He calls out, innocently, musically: "Who's theeeeere?"

"Me, motherfucker! Open up!"

Yogi and Margarita trade looks. Lil' Sleeper's eyes bulge. He looks like he's about to throw up.

Five years ago, when Lil' Sleeper was still known as David and was about to be jumped into the gang, he went to Sleeper and asked him could he have his name. It is a common tradition, like adoption in reverse. Sleeper was honored. And he was willing. But there was a problem—another homeboy was *already* calling himself Lil' Sleeper. The thing was, that Lil' Sleeper had turned out to be a cheese eater. Sleeper was sorry he'd ever said yes to that *vato*. So if David wanted the handle for himself, Sleeper told him, he could have it. But first, he would have to beat up the other Lil' Sleeper and take the name away from him.

The fight was bloody but short. David became Lil' Sleeper. Thereafter, he owed his allegiance to Sleeper.

Now Lil' Sleeper chews on his thumb, trying to think. "Open the door," he says at last.

Sleeper is hype. And he's even more pissed for being made to wait outside Yogi's bedroom door like some, like some... *What the fuck, ese*? His jaw is clenched. The veins in his neck are tight. He points a dirty calloused finger at his namesake. "What have you done to pay back Culver City?" he demands.

Lil' Sleeper looks up at him defiantly. "We ain't gonna do *nothing*" he says.

"We ain't gonna do *nothing*," Yogi repeats. He's got his homey's back. Little Banditos 4-ever.

"You got shot at the other day in your own neighborhood, homeboy! You got shot at *three times* in one week!"

Lil' Sleeper shrugs. "Why's it up to *me* to do something? There's other people who live here, too."

Sleeper stares at him in disbelief. *Can you believe this punk*? Then his eyes drift down to the carpet. There are lots of little white pieces of paper and lint and cloth and cigarette ash down there. To him, each piece looks like a rock. Could be a rock. He wants to reach down and...

"Gimme a blast," Sleeper demands. His lips are pulled back in a tight grimace.

"We was just going to get a ten from Binky," Yogi says.

"A ten?" Sleeper chews his thumb, considering.

Yogi brightens. "Maybe we could get him to kick us down a little more."

"Hand me that pipe," Sleeper says. "Is there any residue in there?"

"What about Culver City?" asks Margarita.

"We'll get them later," Sleeper says.

The High Life and Strange Times of the Pope of Pot

There's a knock at the door and Mickey the Pope, the Pope of Pot, stubs out a joint and stashes it in a drawer. "Gotta go now, toots," he rasps, smoke leaking from his chipmunk grin, and then he laughs, "Ah-ha-ha-HA!" and then he coughs, a deep black hack that shudders his shoulders. He swallows hard, wipes a tear, shrugs and smiles. A trickle of blood reddens the groove between his two front teeth.

Mickey hangs up the phone, writes a number in his little book with a green pen. His entries aren't alphabetical—more experiential, like life, taken in the order that comes, always in alternating colors. He likes things around him to be beautiful, the way God intended. He closes the book, puts a finger to his lips, concentrates. Something to do... What was it?... Hmmm...

Mickey pans the room, in search of a clue: refrigerator, a stack of chairs, a poster of the Italian rock & roller he has taken off the street, a hot plate with one coil glowing, his desk, a pile of bills, a birthday card. *Birthday!* Today is Mickey the Pope's birthday. He is forty-nine years old. Today is also the day before the winter solstice, the last shortening day on the calendar of seasons. This is significant somehow to Mickey the Pope, who's facing fifteen years in the slammer.

Since the bust, sales are down by more than half. Expenses, however, remain the same. It looks like Mickey will have to get a loan. He'll have to ask his little brother to cosign. His brother, of course, will insist that Mickey write something besides *pope* on the section marked EMPLOYMENT. He thinks Mickey is *meshugge*. He may be right. But the fact is, Mickey can't stop being pope just because he has no money. When you start your own church, take the top spot, register it with the City of New York, you make a lifetime commitment. You have responsibilities, toots: You have to tend the flock, buy and dispense sacrament, hire couriers—people you can trust. And then there is operations: two apartments, two offices, the church, the handouts to unfortunates, the food and the dental plan for employees, the telephone lines, 800-WANT-POT. Give the pope a call if you live in Manhattan. Leave your address, your first name, a description of yourself. Your pot will arrive by bicycle in forty minutes or less.

Mickey spies his papal miter—a high, white, John Paul crown, with underwires shaped to a peak, a nine-inch marijuana leaf pasted on the front, lace trailing from the sides. He dons it, trying the polka-dot ribbon beneath his chin. He wears the miter for all public appearances. The May Day Smoke-In at Washington Square, the Halloween parade in Greenwich Village, ACT-UP demonstrations at City Hall, Wigstock, in Tompkins Square—any occasion that requires his high-camp popely presence, any opportunity to stroll the streets, preach the gospel of marijuana and hand out free joints, the sacrament of his Church of Realized Fantasies.

Mickey the Pope swivels around in his chair, grinning, mouth agape, glasses glinting in the fluorescent light. "Ah-ha-ha-HA!"

The door again. Knock, knock.

Oh, yeah. The door. It is made of metal. It is very heavy. Mickey shambles over and yanks. His arm boings like a rubber band. The door doesn't budge.

Mickey giggles and shrugs. What, me worry? Used to be Mickey weighed 300 pounds. He's down a bit lately. A lot. He's a little weak. This diabetes shit. The bleeding gums, the fading eyesight. And all the time drink-and-piss, drink-and-piss, the other day he wet his pants. It was an accident. People have accidents. It'll be all right. The winter solstice is upon us, and the days will be longer, the world will be brighter. This is nature. We know this for a fact. Just as we know that when his church hits 1 million members, he'll have the best medical care available. Just as we know that when his case comes up, the jury will acquit. Some juror, the pope is sure, will know what he knows: that to follow an insane law is to be insane yourself.

Things may look bleak, but Mickey the Pope will find his way clear. He always has. He speaks with the voice and the authority of God. He'll tell you that himself. He also has experience on his side. Twenty years in the pot business, a dozen arrests, seven gunshot wounds, three years in jails, one deportation and all those men, toots, so many wonderful, beautiful men. The counselors at camp. The kids in his bunk. Ten percent of the crew of the U.S. Navy carrier *Intrepid* in the spring and summer of 1959. Two at once on public-access television, a salt-and-pepper team, the black one so big he could do it to himself if he wanted.

And then there was the guy in Amsterdam. He was hired to kill Mickey. As it was, Mickey was just wounded. Mickey was really fat then. The shot passed through the fleshy part of his right arm, down into his belly and out again. What Mickey remembers is that oil oozed from the wounds. It looked like chicken fat, nice and bright and yellow. "I felt like an oil sheik," he says. "*Ah-ha-ha-HA!*"

In the end, the guy who tried to kill him in Amsterdam became another of the many and varied lovers of Mickey the Pope. Amsterdam: that was the place, those were the days. During the Seventies, Mickey the Pope was known in Amsterdam as *Da Paus Maus*. He was the No. 1 pot dealer in a city of heads, unloading nickels, dimes, lids, to the tune of seven kilos a day, selling out of a room in his five-story houseboat on the Amstel River, the front hatch of which was painted to resemble a giant pair of red lips. You had to come through the lips to meet the pope.

The knock again. Mickey the Pope pulls hard on the door.

Late December in the meatpacking district in New York, the sunlight leaning into the West Side afternoon. In a few hours the crack boys will stir and the curbs will be deep in transvestites, and effeminate men wearing leathers and lots of keys will come jangling down the block holding hands, headed for a basement club called the Hellfire. Now, though, things are almost serene on this corner of Thirteenth and Hudson, just in sight of the river. Mothers push strollers, delivery trucks come and go, old Irish ladies promenade—constitutionals taken daily since the boom days on the waterfront, when corners like Mickey's were given over to pubs.

The pope's place, his Church of Realized Fantasies, is painted yellow in its present incarnation, a bright beacon against dark, slick streets and dirty brick. It's an old comic-book store—Dick Tracy painted on one side—with eight big windows, so good for his plants. Mickey the Pope loves plants.

Two men stand flat-footed outside the church. One wears a pompadour and a trench coat. He looks like a mobster. The other carries a pad. He looks like a balding Irish guy in a leather jacket trying to look like something other than a cop. The door swings open. "Michael Cezar?" asks the guy in the leather jacket.

"Howdy, honey, howdy!" rasps Mickey the Pope, beak nose, red faced, wearing his marijuana bonnet. He giggles, raises his hands—palms out—and rubs tiny circles in the air before him, the papal greeting.

"Internal Affairs," says the guy in the pompadour.

* * *

Back now to August, earlier in the year. Across the Americas, from Bogotá to Harlem, the drug war is raging. Though the government has proclaimed drug use on the slide, curb-side dealers are trading briskly in cocaine, prices are down, supply stable, the rat-a-tat-tat of automatic-weapons fire rings across the ghettos like cash-register bells. Sales are also strong in heroin, an old drug making a resurgence as an antidote to crack. At first the police notice a sudden infusion of high-grade, low-price H into the cities. Later it is revealed, but not widely reported, that most of the stuff is China White from Asia's Golden Triangle, moved into America by Triads, many of whose members have recently emigrated from Hong Kong. What fools the police is ingenuity: Chemists are processing different batches with different recipes out of the international heroin cookbook, making some of it look like Mexican, some like Lebanese.

Meanwhile, potheads across the mainland are mourning. It is the time of the drought, the great marijuana drought of 1990, the summer of scrounging, of smoking roaches and cleaning seeds and finally just giving up. Film at eleven shows bonfires of prime buds and old tires sending thick black smoke into the ecosystem. County sheriffs in camouflage fatigues stand around smiling, pitchforks or shotguns in hand. In the cities, the police and legislators launch a massive assault on head shops. Mail-order companies are also targeted. The police seize records, mailing lists, stock. It becomes impossible to buy a bong.

One fine summer day in the midst of all this, a New York radio personality named Howard Stern—the drive-time attitude idol of the bridge-and-tunnel crowd—is sitting at his desk at the station. He's paging through a New Jersey newspaper, looking for material for his talk show, when he spies an ad. He blinks in disbelief.

"Call 1-800-WANT-POT."

The next morning, live before 2 million listeners in three Eastern cities, Howard calls Mickey the Pope.

"Hey, dude!" Howard says. "You're on the air!"

"Howdy, honey, howdy!" rasps Mickey. "I'm the pope. The Church of Realized Fantasies."

"So what do you do, sell pot?"

"Oh... see..." says Mickey. "We give out sacrament for those who need it."

"You don't think it causes any—"

"No," interrupts the pope. "It cures everything. Even AIDS."

"It gives you breasts," blurts Howard. "How's your breasts?"

"My breath may stink a little. I didn't brush my teeth."

"No! Your breasts!"

"They're fine," says the pope. "They get erect, I suppose."

"So," says Howard, changing the subject. "You make a lot of money doing this?"

"I'm living on the Upper East Side. I'm comfy. And I have a palace in New Jersey."

"Really? All from just dealing pot?"

"Well, from being the pope. A lot of people admire the pope."

They talk a while longer, then Howard says goodbye.

"You know," Howard says to his sidekick, Robin Quivers, "I had seen the number in the newspaper, and I thought, 'This is kinda cool.' I mean, I don't think it's cool that he's a drug dealer, but it's kinda cool that he's getting away with it."

"It seems it would be pretty easy to catch him, wouldn't it?" says Robin. "You just call him up, make an order, he shows up, you book him."

"He ought to change his number to 1-800-ARREST-ME," says Howard.

* * *

Mickey the Pope was born Michael Ellis Cezar, In New York City's Greenwich Village, the eldest child of a Jewish engineer and his wife, the daughter of a former postmaster general of Jamaica who was the scion of an English colonial family that had made a fortune mining bauxite. Mickey's father owned an electronics factory in Paterson, New Jersey, which built transformers for radar, the space program, nuclear-power plants. Mickey's little brother runs the factory today. One sister is a real-estate agent; the other, a ceramics teacher who lives in the family "palace," a large house in Morris Plains, New Jersey, which has been stripped of all its furnishings to pay the family bills.

Mickey dropped out of high school after his father went bankrupt. Starting over in a new plant, Mickey built tables for machines, hooked up the electric and the plumbing, did everything from filing and drilling to sweeping the floor. Later, after a stint in the navy, he feuded with his father, who in turn disinherited his son and committed him to a mental institution. Upon his release, Mickey fled to Europe.

One day in the early Seventies, Mickey took the fabled Magic Bus Tour of Amsterdam. When it stopped at the Lowlands Weed Company, says Mickey, "I knew I'd found a home."

Lowlands Weed, it turned out, was owned by a bunch of Dutch Provos, anarchists who renounced the concept of work. They were known for their be-ins, demonstrations during which they sat around and did nothing but be themselves. The Provos also advocated the legalization of marijuana. They were the original potheads of Europe, the Continent's largest dealers. They would eventually place several of their number on Amsterdam's city council. Oddly, after achieving their political foothold, the Provos disbanded. It was probably the shock. Having won, these devout anarchists found themselves in charge of legislating societal order.

"They were a bunch of crazy people," says Mickey the Pope. "This one guy threw smoke bombs at the marriage of some Dutch aristocrat. He used to have sex with women and their kids. I'm telling the truth. I had people take shits on my floor. I had other people come in and eat it.

"In the beginning, they sold pot by the plant and seeds," the pope continues. "I convinced them to sell the smokable product. Buses would pull up and three-quarters of the passengers would flow into the shop to buy pot."

Soon, *Da Paus Maus* moved out of Lowlands and founded his own retail operation, selling out of a series of ever-larger houseboats. A port city, Amsterdam had an almost inexhaustible supply of drugs. *Da Paus* would get the list of ships from the harbor master, then go down to the docks at three in the morning. He'd fall into step with some sailors, say, "Howdy, toots!" and offer to share a joint.

"And then you'd go on board and there were tons of smoke pouring out of the ship," Mickey says. "Everybody had the stuff. So I'd give them a good price and they'd throw it down on the dock, and then I'd drive out, waving to the customs guy. He knew everything. The whole government was in on it. I was once visited on my houseboat by some secretary of state. He said, 'Keep up the good work. It's great for the tourists!'"

Amsterdam had always been known for its coffee bars and hashish, but the pope saw an opening and set about creating a market for marijuana. He kept long hours, stayed open seven days a week and sold at a tiny profit—even advertised in the yellow pages as "Hennep Producten." Pretty soon, says the pope, the Cosmos, the Milkyway, Paradiso, all the big clubs were selling Mickey's finest. "I was making, like, $20,000 a day," remembers Mickey.

Mickey lived the good life for a while, spending the guilders as fast as they came in. He bought a new boat, an old school to house his forty workers. He even paid for medical and dental plans. Then *Da Paus Maus* was busted. After seven years in business, Mickey was kicked out of Holland.

Penniless, still estranged from his family, Mickey landed on New York's Lower East Side in 1979. He met up with some anarchists, moved into a little apartment at First Street and First Avenue and began selling loose joints. Soon he started his first telephone delivery service, 777-CASH.

And thus began the pope's delivery empire. He serviced UN diplomats, rock stars, whorehouses, nightclubs, night watchmen, magazine editors, yippies, yuppies and punks. For a time the pope had a diner. For a time he operated a storefront on First Street, selling bags brazenly to all comers. When that store was busted in 1981, the pope did eight months in Rikers Island Prison, whereupon he returned to the Lower East Side and started all over again, this time at Eleventh Street and Avenue B.

"People lined up outside to buy pot all day long," says a longtime associate. "They were taking the money out in garbage bags, but the cops were so busy with all the heroin in the neighborhood they didn't really have time to fool with Mickey."

The mid-Eighties saw the pope battling the underworld. First came a Puerto Rican gang called the Hitmen Club. When Mickey refused to pay protection money, the gang members forced their way into his telephone center, holding the workers at bay with a .357 and a straight razor, taking $500. The next day they came back, demanding $1,000 a week from the pope. When Mickey refused, they ambushed him later on the street, shooting him six times with a .22. "He was so fat they didn't hit any vital organs," say the associate. "The ambulance guy didn't even believe Mickey had been shot until he opened up his coat and showed him the bullet holes."

Later the young sons of some Italian mobsters would try to muscle in on Mickey's operations. They cut the phone lines, waited outside to break Mickey's legs. Meanwhile, inside, Mickey the Pope was alone, in pain from a bowel obstruction, a complication from the Puerto Rican ambush. Weak, sick, determined, he held the fort for five days. In the end he was rescued by his father. "Well, I guess if you're dying, I can take you to the hospital," the old man said.

Over the years, Mickey estimates, he has presided over phone operations in more than forty different locations, always with modest success. Then came the summer of 1990, the drought. Nobody could find any pot except for Mickey. Business boomed.

Each morning, the bicycle couriers would meet at a secret location and check out stock for the day, four-gram bags of brown-green commercial Mexican, packaged in sealable glassine inside white paper envelopes. The couriers would hit the streets by 10:00 a.m. As calls came in, telephone operators would take down locations in logbooks and then beep the couriers, who would deliver the goods within forty minutes. Each bag cost the consumer $50. Delivery was $10 extra. At twenty-eight grams to the ounce, the pope's medium-grade pot was expensive, selling at about $350 a lid. But it was the only pot available. One hundred or 200 calls a day were not unusual.

By eight each morning, the couriers would check back in and pay up. No business was done after dark. That's when the real criminals were out, and couriers were often taken down by street thugs or fake cops with Chinatown shields. Mickey worried for his people. Usually, at night, the pope would gather around him a number of his flock and somebody would cook a big dinner. It was a happy family, mostly. And why not? The pope provided food, a dental plan, money to fix a broken bike. He gave out free pot, sometimes paid the medical bills of people he knew with AIDS. He'd even let you live in the telephone center or his extra apartment if you needed a place to squat. The police say Mickey was doing $40,000 a day. Mickey says he was probably making about half that much.

In any case, as quick as it came, it went. As Mickey says, "Money is like manure, toots, it's meant to be spread around."

Then, just as the church was hitting its stride, the New York police did exactly what Robin and Howard had suggested on their radio show. On September 22nd, 1990, the cops called the pope's 800 number. As guaranteed, a courier delivered. The police did the same again on October 12th and 26th. A few days later, during the massive Halloween parade held each year in the West Village, the pope gave a joint to an undercover cop. Handing it over—as he had to so many others that evening—Mickey giggled and declared: "I'm the Pope of Pot! If you want pot, call my number!"

That was it. The NYPD labeled Mickey the Pope a high priority. "There comes a time when you have to let people know that you are serious," said Special Narcotics Prosecutor

Sterling Johnson. "He defied the authorities. He threw down the gauntlet."

On November 14th, with the press in tow, the cops raided the Pope of Pot. It was, said the *Village Voice*, "a police operation worthy of *America's Most Wanted*." The bust made all the news shows the next day and all the papers, even the *New York Times*. The *New York Post* played it on the front page with the headline COPS NAB PHONE 'POPE OF DOPE.' Police officials were quoted as saying that Mickey was taking 360 calls an hour on six telephones.

Mickey was brought out of his yellow church to a fusillade of flashbulbs and questions. Handcuffed, red faced, blood pressure roaring, the pope had time to rasp only a quick, "Howdy, honey, howdy," before he was piled into a police car. Over in the shadows across the street, crack dealers and transvestites watched in amazement. They knew Mickey. On cold nights, he sometimes let them into the church to get warm. He gave out hot chocolate.

Then a cop in a suit, Assistant Chief John J. Hill, stepped forward into the klieg lights. His public statement: "We seized here a total of five messengers, two people operating the phones and the pope himself. Also seized were seven pounds of marijuana."

* * *

Nighttime now at the Church of Realized Fantasies. In an hour or two the doors will open at a club called Mars, and a benefit will commence, a bailout throw-down for Mickey the Pope. Meantime, some of the inner circle have gathered to wait. They smoke joints, watch a video of the pope, eat sponge-cake, drink hot chocolate.

Soon after his arrest and release, Mickey was arrested again, this time for participating in an ACT-UP protest. Radical gays, demonstrating for a city-sponsored needle exchange for addicts, collected dirty syringes in a bucket. The pope was snatched when he attempted to turn the needles over to the police. Later he was arrested again for selling a half an ounce of pot to an undercover cop who came calling at the "palace" in New Jersey.

So it has gone. At the moment, the Pope of Pot is, to put it simply, destitute. All the change from the Mason jar in his apartment has been spent. He doesn't even have a subway token in his pocket. He has plenty of church currency—poker chips in various colors stamped in gold with his sickle and marijuana leaf insignia—but nobody wants it. MCI has cut off the 800 number; New York Tel is threatening his other accounts. Landlords are clamoring too. And, of course, there are the lawyers.

Hence the benefit, this gathering at Mickey's church. They are an odd bunch sitting on stackable plastic chairs, about two dozen of the 5,000 that Mickey claims as followers, having crawled this night from the belly of an F train from the Lower East Side, descendants of Burroughs and Ginsberg and Huncke and Junkie, of Madonna, Andy Warhol and Kenny Scharf, the ever-changing members of the cult of near-fatal hipness that has thrived for so long in the East Village.

There's a guy in a Burberry raincoat, a silk tie, one eye stitched shut. A Russian Jew. A singer who is famous for looking like John Lennon. A man who looks like Charles Manson. A man named Mighty Man. One guy wears a black turban and little, square red plastic sunglasses. Another wears striped pants, a plaid coat, a Siberian fur hat. No one says a thing. Not a word. They sit, dumb, passing a joint.

Over in a corner, near the hot plate that heats the storefront, Mickey the Pope is being videoed as he watches the video of himself on a TV. An artist named Clayton has the minicam. He takes the thing everywhere, its red eye glowing, recording for a documentary what's been known for years in its many and varied forms as "the scene." Clayton made headlines in 1988 when he refused to surrender some footage to city authorities. His film showed cops, badges removed, beating homeless men and local residents with nightsticks during a riot in Tompkins Square Park. Clayton also has a storefront on the Lower East Side, on

Essex below Houston, next to a kosher Chinese restaurant, in a Puerto Rican neighborhood known to Caucasian druggies from New Jersey as a good copping spot for Percodan. Clayton's mustache looks like two caterpillars inching along his lip line toward his nose. His goatee is long and thin like one of the Three Musketeers'. The hair along his two frontal lobes has been shaved. The rest hangs long in the back.

To Clayton's left is Mickey the Pope, who is being pumped by a woman for information about a friend of hers named Danny Rakowitz. Rakowitz is a Lower East Side artist and short-order cook who was arrested for cutting up his girlfriend, cooking her into soup, serving the soup to the homeless, leaving her skull and bones in a five-gallon bucket filled with Kitty Litter in the baggage claim at the bus station.

Rakowitz's friend is a tiny black woman with ashen skin and a shock of nappy hair. Her leather jacket is decorated with skull buttons. She looks like a skull, all cheekbones and sunken eyes and this thick top lip that flies up and to the left with every third word, a dancing sneer, a sort of visual "Fuck you." She is sure her friend didn't kill Monica. She's been interviewing people for months, gathering evidence. There's a plot. She knows this. Everyone is involved.

"But Danny had no reason to kill Monica," declares the skull lady. "What's the difference?" asks the pope. "The girl saw the body in the bathtub."

"Doesn't that seem strange to you?"

"Of course it does."

"Why wasn't there any blood?" asks skull lady. "Where was the blood?"

"An awful lot of cleaning, dear," says the pope, lecturing. "Put her in the tub. Cut her up. Run the water, toots. Ah-ha-ha-HA!" He raises his palms, rubs tiny circles in the air before him. "The guy is crazy. He even had a sign on the door: SOUP KITCHEN. Everybody knew it."

"Well, why didn't anybody call the cops?"

"Why didn't anyone call the cops?" repeats the pope, begging the question. He snorts and giggles. "What do you expect? It's the Lower East Side."

* * *

Only in New York, only on the Lower East Side, could somebody like the pope be the pope.

Three centuries ago, the Lower East Side was farmland and aboriginal hardwood forest, and the Bowery—now the western edge of the district, changing to Third Avenue just north of Houston Street—was a trail, used by Native Americans in their sorties against the occupying Dutch colony of New Amsterdam. Today, this jumble of factories, tenements and storefronts, strewn from Astor Place to Alphabet City and from Fourteenth Street to Chinatown, remains the wilds of Manhattan—a campground from which the natives, with their alternative lifestyles, still launch assaults on the tastes of the mainstream uptown.

The late 1800s on the Lower East Side saw the first flowering of the immigrants. Millions of Turks, Greeks, Italians, Poles, Germans, Ukrainians and Jews came through Ellis Island to the world's newest urban frontier. It was a dense ethnic soup, the original American pepper pot—a world, according to a WPA guidebook, "of politicians, artists, gangsters, composers, prizefighters and labor leaders."

World War II, the Fifties, the early Sixties, saw new waves of immigration. Jews gave way to Puerto Ricans, winos and junkies. The Beat era was upon the East Village, a dark time of morphine, heroin and speed, of caffeine and marijuana, of bongos, berets, turtlenecks and homosexuality. Starting with writers William Burroughs and Herbert Huncke, poet Allen Ginsberg—continuing with Jack Kerouac, Neal Cassady, the Merry Pranksters, hallucinogens, communal living, free love—a new kind of culture, expressed in the widest range of perverse and irreverent and star-crossed possibilities, grew in the shabby far reaches of the Lower East Side.

The Seventies saw the rise of the club and art scene. There were punk rockers, hip-hoppers, new wavers, performance artists, fashion designers and drag queens. The club of the moment was CBGB; the musicians were Lou Reed, Patti Smith, Debbie Harry, the Ramones. Andy Warhol and his Factory were the spiritual center of the art world. Around him would revolve the likes of Keith Haring and Jean-Michel Basquiat.

"Although they sprang from varied backgrounds, the artists [who came to the area] shared a collective media-drenched consciousness, the heritage of the suburban teenager," writes Steven Hager in his book about the East Village. "In the Sixties, this pampered upbringing was frequently a source of guilt, but in the Seventies, it was dissected and rearranged, and eventually regurgitated into new forms."

In the last few years, with the fall of the economy and the rise of a new era of American Prohibition, the Lower East Side has hit hard and seamy times. "Every year it's been a different thing," says Clayton, the video artist. "Some years it's been drag queens. Other years it's been skinheads, the police, squatters, homeless. This year seems to be, you know, there's a depression happening in the country, a lot of uncertainty. They're trying to close our fire department, that's big for us. There's Mickey's bust, the Rakowitz murder, AIDS, crack. It changes down here, but it never changes. A lot of these fuckin' people are geniuses. A lot of them are nuts."

* * *

"So what's up with the telephone center," asks the hippie. "Is it cool or not?"

"I don't know," says Mickey the Pope.

"Well, we're only doing twenty deliveries a day, and that ain't shit!"

"Put me on PR!" chimes in Bartman. "Give me a minimum budget! Give me no budget!"

The pope eyes Bartman, shakes his head in sorrow. Bartman, Freddie Redpants, Larry the Libertarian... Why can't he find some help? Why must he do everything himself? Here in the church, a few days before his birthday, Mickey the Pope is in ruins. The other night at the fund-raiser at Mars, 700 people crowded all four floors. It was a raging success. There was so much support for the pope that you couldn't move across the room. Unfortunately, nobody at the benefit thought about collecting any money.

In the end, Mickey the Pope lost forty dollars.

So now he has gotten himself a new partner. Call him the hippie. He is bald on top with a fringe of shoulder-length hair, a gray beard cascading down his chest. He is hyper, creepy. He keeps looking all around him. Toward the windows. The back room. Under the papers on Mickey's desk. "So what about the phone center?" he asks again, picking up the trash can, checking the bottom, putting it back down. "Is it cool?"

"Well, there wasn't a big investigation," interrupts Bartman. "They didn't freeze his bank accounts. It was just—"

"Baaaaaaart!" chides the pope.

"Listen, you little turd!" says the hippie, eyes suddenly wild, finger in Bartman's nose. "What you gotta do is one thing. Meet Red each morning, pick up, work. No talking. Got it?

"I've cut back about twenty percent," says Bartman. "I'm definitely talking less. I'm gonna—"

"You're gonna do what you got to do!" hollers the hippie, puffing up, ballistic, a vein popping in his right temple. He zeros in on the hapless Bartman: "Look. I got a lot going for me right now. I can't have some little pussy to fuck it up. If I'm gonna go to jail for conspiracy, I'll kill a fucker and go to jail for the same amount of time!"

"I'm with that!" says Bartman.

"You know what I'm sayin'?" asks the hippie.

"Fuck! I swear!"

"Now, now, boys, boys," says the pope, batting his eyelashes, an aging coquette with curly gray beard. "This is the sacrament we're talking about Please… Respect. *Ah-ha-ha-HA!*"

* * *

The pope is at home now, his Upper East Side studio, a second-floor walkup. He's not feeling too well, lying shirtless on his unmade bed amid a clutter of plants and clothes and videos with titles like *Hot Rocks II*, his scars and bullet wounds looking pink and ropy amid the forest of fine graying hairs covering his torso.

Over in the kitchen, a friend of the pope's is scouring the oven. The sink is filled with dishes. A flesh-colored marital aid pokes up out of the soapsuds. The friend has just been released after twenty years in prison. He doesn't want his name mentioned, but he intimates that he had something to do with an art heist and a murder at a big museum in New York City. He met the pope in prison. All the Jewish guys there knew each other. He looked out for the pope. They also took ceramics together. The pope is letting him crash in a basement apartment while he looks for a job in his old field, public relations.

It is time now for a papal audience. Why? The pope is asked. Why is he setting up business anew? Why is he letting a reporter see all this? Does he have to have an 800 number? Couldn't he just chill like the other eleven delivery services in Manhattan, do a thriving underground business? Perhaps Howard Stern is right. Is he begging to go to jail?

"I'm the bringer of wisdom and truth," explains Mickey the Pope. "I'm doing what's right. I'm the kind of person, you're not gonna intimidate me. Marijuana is the saving plant. It should be legal. People want it that way. The voice of the people is the voice of God in a democracy. If you get enough people into it, the politicians have to listen. I think what we should do is, sort of set up our own society and do our own thing. Let all the others go do what they will. We're doing what's right and proper and screw 'em, our little group should live better than they do. We should win by example."

With that the tape recorder clicks off. The pope takes a long slow drink from a gallon jug of water, then grins, bats his lashes. "So how'd I do, toots?" he asks. "This is serious. I don't want to go to jail. I really don't want to go to jail."

* * *

Now it is Mickey the Pope's birthday, the day before the winter solstice, the last shortening day on the calendar of the seasons. There's a knock at the church door, and Mickey opens up and finds two undercover cops. One wears a pompadour and a trench coat. The other carries a pad.

"Oh! Internal Affairs!" giggles Mickey the Pope. "I called you, didn't I?"

"Yes, sir," says the cop with the pad. He regards Mickey for a moment, beak nosed, red faced, wearing his marijuana bonnet. The cop rolls his eyes to the heavens. "Mind if we come in?"

"Of course, toots," rasps the pope, bowing, gesturing, showing the guests to some chairs.

"So what happened?" asks the cop with the pad.

"Well, when I was busted, there was this big media thing, you know, and John J. Hill said there were seven pounds confiscated in the raid."

"John J. Hill?" asks the pad.

"Yeah, he's an assistant chief."

"Oh! Chief Hill!" exclaims the pompadour, leaning forward.

"He said there were seven pounds?" asks the pad.

"Right there on the news," says Mickey.

"Oh," says the pompadour.

"So how many pounds were there?" asks the pad.

"Close to five."

"So, close to five pounds were taken into evidence by the police?"

"Right," says the pope.

"So, what's the problem?" asks the pompadour.

"Well, I was only indicted for two and one half pounds."

"So what's the problem?" asks the pad.

"See," says the pope, grinning. "Two and one half pounds are missing! Cops shouldn't be stealing the evidence. I mean, I don't steal. I don't jump turnstiles, none of that shit. I really don't. I live the pure life. I don't take from nobody, and that's the truth."

"I see," says the pompadour.

"The thing is, if the cops want pot, they should have to buy it like everyone else," says the pope. "If you're not gonna charge me for it. I want it back. After all, it's the sacrament. This is the church. The marijuana church. The Church of Realized Fantasies."

The Real Rick Ross is Not a Rapper

The real Rick Ross is not a rapper. That's what it says on his T-shirt, silk-screened attractively in two colors. The bold letters in black ink frame his image – bald, bearded, and somewhat bug-eyed with the fervor of his comeback. The gold ink requires a second stencil. Depicted on his head is a crown, cocked just so and perfectly aligned, the kingpin in exile, and below that his autograph, the excessively flamboyant signature of a man who once made millions a day selling cocaine but only began learning to read, behind bars, at age twenty-eight. Eventually he would read himself to freedom.

On a sunny morning in southern California, Rick Ross is driving from his cramped but rent-free apartment along tony Ocean Avenue in Long Beach toward some pressing new business in blue-collar Riverside, an hour away. We're talking here about the real Rick Ross, born Ricky Donnell Ross in 1960, one of three Ricks from 'round the way, this one the Rick who stayed on Eighty-seventh Place where it dead-ended at the 110 Freeway, in the shadow of a massive concrete abutment where you could feel the earth vibrating beneath your feet, hence his nickname: Freeway Rick Ross... as opposed to the rapper known as Rick

Ross, a blubbery former college football player and corrections officer whose birth name is William Leonard Roberts II. When Roberts entered the music game, he appropriated the name and tattooed it across his fists: RICK RO$$. He rose to prominence rapping about a fictitious criminal past while the real Rick Ross, Freeway Rick Ross, a man iconic enough to have his name jacked, was serving a life sentence without the possibility of parole in a federal penitentiary.

Having brought suit against the rapper for copyright infringement and failed in several courts, Ross came up with the idea of these T-shirts. Over the past five months, with the help of a gangbanger turned silk-screener, he's printed five thousand. Offered in a rainbow of colors, in sizes up to 6XL, they are folded painstakingly and fitted into plastic bags by his older brother in a mini-warehouse to which Ross has managed to secure the key, one in a seemingly endless series of fuzzy handshake arrangements through which he operates his portfolio of legal enterprises.

Everywhere he goes—to give testimony in a storefront church in Ontario; to lecture a law-school class at the University of Southern California; to make a personal appearance at an open-mic night in Inglewood; to have lunch at Denny's in Carson (he's a vegan; the chain features a garden burger); to attend a party for a Korean rapper who worships Ross as an American folk hero; to take a meeting at Warner Bros. studios in Burbank or with an Epic/Sony vice-president in Beverly Hills—Ross rolls behind him unselfconsciously a battered suitcase full of merch, the zipper toggles missing, his Willy Loman smile unwavering as he digs through the slippery packages to find the proper size and color, no charge for a photo. If you don't have the twenty dollars, more than likely he'll sell it for less. Taken by the moment, by the recognition and adulation, he'll often make it a gift.

If you meet Rick Ross and you tell him you're broke, broker even than he is at the moment — there is $11.15 left in his savings account—he'll spot you a ten-pack of T-shirts, a $200 value on the streets. (If you live out of town, he'll mail you a ten-pack; someone else donates postage from his company's postal machine.) His manufacturer's price is about four dollars per piece. Wholesale is ten dollars. On the Web the price is twenty-five dollars. Sell those shirts, pay him back a hundred dollars, and you get to keep the profit. If you're smart like Rick Ross, the real Rick Ross, Freeway Rick, you'll reinvest. Just like that you're in business.

Back in the day, Ross would offer the same deal with crack cocaine — to start you out, he'd give you $100 worth for free and you could sell it for $300. Between 1982 and 1989, federal prosecutors estimated, Ross bought and resold *three tons* of cocaine. In 1980 dollars, his gross earnings were said to be in excess of $900 million — with a profit of nearly $300 million. Converted roughly to present-day dollars: $2.5 billion and $850 million, respectively. As his distribution empire grew to include forty-two cities, the price he paid per kilo of powder cocaine dropped from as much as $60,000 to as low as $10,000. This was partially due to his exponentially increasing network of distributors, as Crips and Bloods struck out across the country to franchise the trade, spreading their gang culture with it... and partially due to his sweetheart connection with a Nicaraguan national who would later be said to have ties to both the CIA and the contra rebels supported during the 1980s by the Reagan administration. (Later this same connect—Oscar Danilo Blandón—would be hired by the DEA as an informant; it was he who would bring Ross into the deal that led to his life sentence.)

Fueled by the findings of an investigation by *San Jose Mercury News* reporter Gary Webb in 1996, many would come to believe that the CIA had actually created the crack epidemic in America by allowing (or turning a blind eye to) massive shipments of cocaine into the country, the profits from which went to arming rebels fighting a Latin American regime disfavored by our government. Webb also theorized that much of the contra coke (cultivated in Colombia) ended up in the hands of Freeway Rick Ross.

Webb's revelations were aggressively attacked by the country's major newspapers, in reports heavy with unnamed government sources. Webb left the paper in disgrace; he was later found dead with two bullets in his head, an apparent suicide. An earlier inquiry led by then-senator John Kerry supported the substance of Webb's allegations, as did a 1998 report by the CIA's inspector general. Even many of those who vilified Webb now acknowledge that much of what he reported was true. A minority of the citizenry still believes there was genocidal intent in the CIA's actions—that the coke was deliberately funneled toward black ghettos as a way of decimating a troublesome population.

Deliberate or not, crack spread like a brush fire through the desiccated urban landscape, causing what USC law professor Jody Armour calls "the crack plague and its festering aftermath." Today, the ripples are still felt on all sociological levels; 30 percent of African-American males under thirty are currently incarcerated or on probation or parole. Along the way, crack also helped to enrich law-enforcement agencies and private security contractors and to elect politicians; being "tough on crime" became a necessary platform plank, a mind-set that would later dovetail into post-9/11 issues of domestic security. In 1986, when homicide rates due to gang warfare across the country had reached all-time highs, mandatory federal sentencing minimums were established, making the penalties for possession of crack by weight a hundred times more punitive than those for possession of powder cocaine. Many say this is one of the reasons for the disparities of race in our prison population. Only recently did President Barack Obama sign legislation reducing the crack-to-powder-coke ratio to 18 to 1. To date, various estimates place the cost of the four-decade-plus war on drugs between $500 billion and $4 trillion.

The way Rick Ross sees it, he was a banker in a shadow economy, working with the only currency available to a disenfranchised segment of society. By giving out unsecured microloans, he created jobs. By middling large quantities of this once-refined plant (similar to sugar or coffee, only illegal), he made himself and others wealthy — an American capitalist in the grand tradition of our country's rags-to-riches folklore. Working with gang leaders he'd known since grade school, both Crips and Bloods, Ross created a sales model — a foolproof recipe for cooking powder coke into crack using household materials; a chain of organization; an army of Dope Boys; and standardized curbside service techniques that were exported around the country and continued to evolve one step ahead of police and their increasingly well-stocked arsenal.

The real Rick Ross. Freeway Rick Ross. He didn't invent crack. But he probably did more than anyone else to cause its spread. Just Say No. The War on Drugs. Mandatory Minimums. *The Wire.* RICK RO$$. This is his legacy. Say hello to my little friend.

* * *

At the moment, Freeway Rick Ross is sitting behind the wheel of a salvaged Hyundai Santa Fe with 169 grand on the odometer. He is traveling seventy miles per hour in the middle lane of the 110 Freeway, heading for the 91 Freeway, chatting nonstop to a series of callers on a BlackBerry cell phone with a cracked face that the mother of his two youngest children — Mychosia Nightingale, a former Army sergeant who did three tours in Iraq — found for him on Craigslist for twenty-nine dollars. (Ross doesn't do computers.)

The steering wheel vibrates beneath his driving hand. The wheels of the vehicle are slightly out of alignment; it was purchased at auction on his behalf by another of his partners, this one a reformed bank robber who is helping him learn the business of flipping low-end cars. So far this week, Ross has sold two cars, one of them the sedan his brother was driving; after repair expenses, he's cleared nearly two grand. There's a nice Honda waiting in Riverside; all it needs is a new air bag and it's ready for Craigslist. Prior to jumping on the freeway, Ross stopped at a junkyard and scored.

By any account, going legit hasn't been easy. After his release from prison in 2009 (more on that below), Ross tried long-distance trucking. He was up to owning seven rigs when the repair bills crippled him. Then, he says, two of his cousins ran off with the last two viable trucks. Next he tried the hair business—human hair for extensions. Another cousin, who was supposed to go to India to buy more hair, ran off with a suitcase full of money.

Ever upbeat, Ross keeps trying. Among projects he's pursuing: a storefront for the T-shirts. A literacy campaign. A social-media campaign (freewaysocialmedia.com). A rap label. (If you want to be signed, you have to sell T-shirts.) A sports training and management agency specializing in troubled athletes. An energy pill. (His potential partner made a fortune selling faux marijuana and bath salts.) By far his biggest hopes lie in Hollywood. Ross has a partnership stake in a documentary about his life, *Crack in the System,* by the filmmaker Marc Levin. He's also shopping his biopic. It was written by Nick Cassavetes, a cowriter of *Blow;* Nick Cannon has signed on to play Freeway Rick Ross. So far Ross hasn't found anyone willing to give him $36 million to make the film.

Likewise the T-shirts. He sold $1,500 worth his first month and reinvested everything. The problem he's got right now is re-ups—he is owed something like $4,000. Apparently, his corps of street salespeople have discovered a slight problem with Ross's model—T-shirts don't sell like crack.

Ross's cell phone is set to speaker, propped on his right shoulder to avoid another ticket. There's a spare battery charging in a broken phone in the cupholder; a third battery floats loose in the pocket of his jeans, the same pair the government issued him on the day he walked out of the federal prison in Texarkana, in northeast Texas, after serving fourteen years of a reduced sentence. The calls come in every few minutes: acolytes and sycophants, old homies and new connects, possible business partners, members of the media.

"What up what up what up?" Ross answers, ever upbeat. "Talk to me. Who dat?"

This particular caller has been highly anticipated. He's from a television show—Russell Brand's late-night talk fest, *Brand X*. The hugely popular English comedian is taping his last installment of the season tonight. Ross is scheduled to appear.

As Rick has been learning, it's one thing to be mobbed by a crowd of adoring brothers and sisters at the giant City of Hope church, or at Earlez Grille on Crenshaw Boulevard, or at the corner of Eighty-first and Hoover, a former weed and PCP spot where Ross became the first street dealer to offer ready rock for sale to the public. (His initial customers were dealers, known as D Boys, the D for dope. They liked to mix a little crack into their marijuana blunts—street name: coco-puffs.)

But it's quite another to gain acceptance from the mainstream — especially when you're trying to raise $36 million for a film. This shot on national TV is just what he needs, a big-time arena in which to push his shirts and his various campaigns, a chance to explain a little bit about himself, to put things in context, to explain his situation—how he was really more of an entrepreneur giving out microloans than a drug pusher peddling death. How the CIA practically put the drugs in his hands.

He puts the caller on speaker. He sounds superfriendly; the two have spoken before. The routine of arrival at the studio is explained. The names of Ross's greenroom entourage are locked down on the list. A medium-sized Real Rick Ross T-shirt is requested. Then talk turns to plans for the segment.

"We'd like to have you show the audience how to make crack," the caller says.

Ross's large and expressive eyes seem to bulge out of their sockets. "You want me... to come on your show and cook crack?" He looks as if he's about to cry.

"Yes!" enthuses the caller. His tone is reminiscent of a cheerleader pumping a fist in the air. "Can you tell me what we'll need?"

* * *

The 110 Freeway links the port of Long Beach with downtown L.A. It runs through the eastern side of the city, paralleling the coastline, passing near the Watts Towers, the L.A. Memorial Coliseum, the USC campus, and the Staples Center before merging with Interstate 10, a gateway to the rest of the nation.

The harbor is one of the world's busiest. Massive ships arrive daily, decks stacked impossibly high with colorful containers, which are unloaded by giant erector-set roustabouts and set like toys onto rail cars and tractor rigs. Leaving Long Beach, the 110, also known as the Harbor Freeway, runs through blighted communities that once housed hundreds of thousands of blue-collar workers, many of them African-Americans who'd immigrated from the South in successive waves after World War II, seeking jobs and a better life. Today the area is best known for gangs, drugs, and economic despair. After the 1992 riots, people of color began to refer to a place called Soweto South of Pico Boulevard—the geographical line of demarcation between the haves and have-nots in Los Angeles.

A number of years ago, the 110 Freeway was widened. By eminent domain, construction claimed the house, at 430 West Eighty-seventh Place, where Ross grew up. Today if you go there, the ground still trembles. Homeless people live in makeshift tents beneath the overpass.

One evening in 1979, when Ross was nineteen and the modest clapboard house still stood, Ross arrived home with his buddy Ollie "Big Loc" Newell to find the usual friends and family hanging out in the garage that Ross and his brother had converted into a bedroom/clubhouse. There was a sofa and chairs, a TV, a rug on the concrete floor.

The house was shared by Ross's aunt and his mother, Annie Mae Mauldin, the daughter of an east-Texas sharecropper, a no-nonsense woman who'd lost her left eye to a broomstick in a fight with a man. Ross's father, Sonny Ross, a former Army cook and later a pig farmer, came from similar roots. Rick would have no relationship with him until after Rick's first stint in prison. He ended up bunking for a time with the old man, the only qualified (and available) non-felon in Texas who was able to offer him shelter under the terms of his release. Having missed out on significant portions of the lives of his own five older children—by far the most painful part of his incarceration, he says—Rick made amends with Sonny before he died. Of particular interest to Ross was the time his dad spent, during his younger days, as a moonshiner. Unlike his son, Sonny tended to quit stuff when it got too hot. (He tried to live in LA for a time but returned after he was held up at gunpoint by two women while working the overnight shift in a gas station in South Central.)

Ross and his mother came to South Central in 1963, when he was three. Left behind in Texas, along with the yellow shack in which he'd grown up, were his brother David, his bicycle, and his dog, Pooch, the things he loved most in the world, according to his autobiography, which he wrote in prison with the help of his cellmate, who helped teach him to read using makeshift flashcards. At first, Ross and his mother lived with her brother, George, and his wife. One night George became enraged and attacked his wife and sister. As little Ricky looked on in terror, his mom pulled a handgun from her purse and killed Uncle George. After what Ross remembers as a long and painful separation, Mauldin was released from jail and mother and son were reunited.

Throwing in with George's wife, Mauldin bought the house on Eighty-seventh Place. Mauldin cleaned office buildings, did landscaping, worked for a lawyer soliciting auto-accident cases. Eventually, the family went on welfare. Ross remembers collecting canned food from looted stores after the Watts riots. Mauldin is now in her mid-eighties, a sprightly woman with a quick laugh who drives a minivan and likes to gamble in a nearby casino. She remembers Ricky being embarrassed by government handouts, always hustling. He cut lawns, sold lemonade, pumped gas for tips, shoplifted, ran errands for neighborhood pimps. At

Manchester Elementary, Ross wasn't so industrious. He fought with classmates, sassed teachers—the little guy with the big temper. Even though he couldn't read, he was promoted every year.

"There weren't no bankers or lawyers in my neighborhood to learn from," Ross says. "The pimps and the hustlers was my role models. There was experts on burglary, there was experts on how to rob somebody at the ATM, how to get a gun, how to file off the serial numbers—all this information was readily available in our community. Criminal enterprise was the only work we had."

As a boy, Ross spent many of his summers back in Texas, on modest farms owned by Mauldin uncles. (For much of his life, Ross hated his name. He wished to be a Mauldin like his cousins.) "If you wanted extra food for dinner, my uncle would tell you okay, but you'd have to put in extra work the next day to pay for it." Later, as a drug dealer, he'd demonstrate the same ethic. "If you called me at twelve o'clock at night, I'd go," he once said. "Another guy, he might be with his girlfriend, 'Oh, I can't come tonight.' Another guy, he be sitting there smoking a cigarette. He can't do nothing until he finish smoking that cigarette. But Rick don't smoke cigarettes. Rick can move right now. He don't have a beer can in his hands or a bottle of liquor. That's the only difference between me and most of my friends in the drug business—my discipline."

Ross attended middle school during the early seventies, around the same time the Crips street gang was being founded by a 17 year old weightlifter named Stanley "Tookie" Williams III. Started initially as a sort of neighborhood-watch brigade by muscleheads who prided themselves on a fly style of dress, the Crips would mutate across South Central (and further spawn the rival Bloods). One day at Bret Harte Junior High, after putting his books into his locker, Ross turned around to find himself staring down the barrel of a .38-caliber pistol—Ross could see clearly the bullet inside the chamber. Somehow his homies defused the incident, but Ross was deeply shaken. He resolved to never join a gang. "I figured there had to be something better for me out there. I just didn't know what it was yet."

As it happened, his answer came in the unlikely form of a tennis racket, when a man showed up to hold a clinic at nearby Manchester Park. Ross went to the park nearly every day, despite the fact that he and his pals had once discovered a mutilated body floating in the swimming pool. (The memory would haunt him for years, as would his uncle's shooting, crippling him at times with debilitating symptoms of post-traumatic shock. In later years Ross would never be known for violence. If someone beat him on a deal, he didn't order a hit. Instead he'd find inspiration, redouble his efforts to succeed. He'd think, *That motherfucker gonna be sorry when I blow the fuck up.*)

At first, given racquets and balls, Ross and his friends ran roughshod across the courts, improvising primitive games of baseball and street hockey. Eventually the instructor prevailed and the ruffians were tamed. Everybody could see it instantly: Freeway Rick had talent.

Too small for football or basketball, the quick and tenacious Ross found in tennis a legit place to excel. By ninth grade he was recruited to play for Dorsey High School, a magnet school in Baldwin Hills, an exclusive residential area south of downtown known as the black Beverly Hills.

Ross climbed the depth chart and eventually garnered all-city honors at Dorsey; he even went so far as to attempt the SATs—a bravado effort that ended dismally. Eventually, he dropped out before receiving his diploma. As his jock friends went off to college scholarships, Ross ended up playing for the tennis team at Los Angeles Trade-Technical College, where he was studying auto upholstery, inspired by his newfound passion for lowriders. He bought a 1966 Impala convertible and set about restoring and customizing it—juiced, lifted, and sporting fancy rims, the vehicle could hop three feet off the ground. He joined a car club and attended regular carhops at Church's Chicken on Vermont Avenue and Century Boulevard. From there, caravans would form, sometimes a mile long—music blaring, cars bouncing, rims gleaming, the rear-ends of some vehicles dragging purposely to create a rooster tail of sparks, called flashing. To pay for his hobby, Ross fell into a network of auto thieves who became known as the Freeway Boys. He also became part owner of a chop shop.

Around the spring of 1982, Ross was arrested for the first time and charged with possession of stolen auto parts. Free on bail and awaiting trial, he got a call, as Ross tells it, from his old friend Mike, a running back who'd left town for a football scholarship to San Jose State University.

Mike was staying in the guesthouse of a nice place in Sugar Hill, an area popular with wealthy black folks prior to Baldwin Hills. It had its own kitchen and everything. Ross had never even had his own room.

Greeting Ross and his boy Ollie at the door, Mike pulled out a plastic baggie filled with white paper bindles. He removed one and opened it—inside was a small amount of white powder that sparkled beneath the lamplight. At the time, the most common drugs to use or sell in the ghetto were black-tar heroin, marijuana, and PCP – phencyclidine, a powerful anesthetic. The only time Ross had even *heard* of cocaine was in the movie *Superfly*.

"This is worth fifty dollars," Mike said.

"Stop lying," Ross laughed.

"Man, no joke. They going crazy over this stuff. All of the entertainers are doing it. All the white people are doing it."

"Well, if it worth that much, I'm gonna find a way to get rich," Ross proclaimed.

"Take this and see what you can do with it," Mike said. He handed over the half-gram bindle.

Now Ross and Ollie arrived home to find the usual suspects collected in the garage bedroom/clubhouse. There was Ross's cousin Kenny, his friends Group and Cruz Dog, a couple of others. In Ross's mind, "these guys was supposed to be the ones in our little circle who knew what was going on in the streets. The players, the down hustlers, the street-smart guys—these was them."

Ollie bolted the interior door and Ross produced with some ceremony the little packet of cocaine. He opened it on the table.

The scent was vaguely medicinal, like something you might smell in the emergency room. Everybody stood dumbfounded, just looking at one another.

Cruz Dog was one of Ross's oldest homies, a fleet wide receiver turned fearless Crip soldier Ross had known since Manchester Elementary.

He pushed back his cap and scratched his head, spoke for the group. "What is it, cuz?"

* * *

Ross and Ollie drove around the 'hood, seeing what they could find out about this new drug, seeking wisdom from elders. They asked an OG named Bonnie and another named Big Al, but they didn't know nothing. Eventually they ran into Martin the pimp. Martin knew all about freebasing. He demonstrated how to cook the powder into crack using baking soda—he produced a small nugget that looked like a white aquarium stone.

Then Martin demonstrated how to smoke it. (It made a loud crackling sound when lit; some say that's the origin of the name.)

An hour later, Ross and Ollie were back at the house on Eighty-seventh Place, stewing on the front porch. The drugs were gone. They owed Mike fifty dollars. Ollie wanted payback.

"Man, you can't kill Martin," Ross said. "That's the OG man, everybody in the 'hood gonna be mad."

Then all of a sudden, Martin pulled up in front of the house. He was riding with Big Mouse, one of the original Crips. The two approached the porch. Martin's eyes looked wide and a little crazy. Ross steeled himself.

The old pimp greeting Ross like a long-lost friend. He took Ross's hand in a soul shake: "Man, I got you a *customer*," he enthused.

When Mike had first pulled out the coke in the guesthouse, Ross snorted a couple of lines and was unimpressed. In powder form the effects were subtle. But after watching Martin cook the crack and compulsively smoke it—and return an hour later in an urgent search for more, with financing in tow—Ross knew he'd discovered an opportunity.Ross wasn't the first to cook and deal crack—a mass-produced form of what others were calling free-base. Crack was documented by UCLA researchers as early as 1974 in the San Francisco area. At the same time Ross was experimenting with sales of ready rock, so were dealers and users in New York and Miami. Along with a source of heat and some water, "a saucer, a glass, a paper towel, and Arm & Hammer baking soda are about all that is needed" to cook crack, according to a physician who testified in 1979 before a U. S. House Select Committee.

In the beginning crack was called freebase. Early crack was the exact same product, only mass produced. (Later Ross would learn, from a leader of the Grape Street Crips, of a substance called "Blow Up" that could be added to the recipe to increase the weight of each batch. With that modification to the process, earnings became exponentially higher—and the quality of the buzz exponentially lower.) An interesting note: At one time, crack had no name. It was considered an unusable by-product. In order to test the purity of a shipment, dealers would cook a batch of crack, a simple chemical procedure, like a high school chemistry experiment demonstrating precipitation. If you cooked a gram of coke with a certain amount of baking soda, and then yielded a half gram of crack (the precipitate was called "come back"), you knew your load was fifty percent pure. Somewhere along the line, someone took stuff out of the trash and tried smoking it. One can only imagine their surprise.

Ross could see immediately that crack had considerable marketing advantages over coke. A five dollar hit created an orgasmic high, somewhat akin to the erotic full body rush of heroin. It also created a powerful urge to chase the first rush every fifteen minutes or so with another hit (interestingly, the Blow Up did not seem to decrease at all the temporal addictive effects). In crack form, coke was no longer water soluble or subject to melting—before the cops got wise, the D Boys would to carry their loose rocks under their tongues to avoid discovery in searches. By 1980, when the comedian Richard Pryor set himself on fire cooking freebase (he preferred a more posh method using ether), the world became aware of this new and dangerous drug. The death of collegiate basketball star Len Bias of a cocaine overdose further moved the drug into prominence. (Crack use was never proven in his case; more likely the Celtics #1 draft choice had been snorting powder.)

At first, Ross middled the coke for Mike, without commission, just to learn the ropes. Then he discovered that his upholstery teacher, who lived in Baldwin Hills, was also into coke. He had connections to Nicaraguan dealers. Ross started buying and selling more and more product. He paid Martin the pimp to cook each batch into crack; in time Ross figured out the simple process himself.

Thereafter, whenever Ross recruited a new subdealer, he'd teach him how to cook. He wasn't afraid to go into a hostile neighborhood to seek out a leader and make a deal. "I wasn't a Crip or a Blood. I was the man with the dope and the opportunity," Ross says.

He'd front as much as a kilo to a new distributor—anything to open a new market. He seemed to have a primitive and almost apriori knowledge of marketing and economics. In his prison-written book he writes of the epiphany of realizing that buying something in bulk was always cheaper than buying only one, a notion unknown to a kid who grew up surviving between welfare checks. Later, Ross would always make sure to stock up on inventory before the first and fifteenth of the month, when the government checks were distributed. He also had the discipline to reinvest his profits. At one point early in the game, Ollie and another guy, who was working with them in partnership, took large chunks of their profit shares and bought brand new vehicles, one a Cadillac, the other a tricked out Ford van. "Instead of buying fancy stuff, I took my money and I went and bought more and more dope—and eventually the dealer told them they was too small time and had to buy their dope from me. So then I was getting a lower price plus I was making money on all they shit, too," Ross explains.

Eventually Ross was introduced to a Nicaraguan named Oscar Danilo Blandón. A former marketing director in Nicaragua, Blandón and his wife were forced to flee their country in 1979 when the Cuban-aided Sandinista rebels defeated the U.S.-trained army of Nicaraguan dictator Anastasio Somoza and took over the country.

Dealing with Blandón, Ross seemed to have virtually unlimited access to drugs. By age twenty-three, Ross says, he was a millionaire; throughout the mid-eighties, he moved hundreds of pounds of cocaine powder a day. "I couldn't sell the shit fast enough. I wanted more, more, more. It's like I was worried it was going to run out," Ross says.

In some respects Ross was the prototypical drug kingpin. He wore a bulletproof vest and carried a 9mm, fathered five babies with four different women, kept himself surrounded by a posse of workers connected by state of the art walkie-talkies, ordered up bootleg designer furnishings for his motel (which he gave to his mom to run), bought an apartment building, sponsored a semipro basketball team, bought new pews for his mom's church, had so much cash he had to hire people to count it—there's a story about his mom finding his stash in his bedroom closet; it took an entire day to count, $2.8 million. After he bought new rims for the basketball courts at Manchester Park, the Los Angeles Department of Recreation and Parks gave him a plaque, expressing "deepest appreciation for your generous donation."

But he was never flashy. Only his intimates knew who he was, what he looked like. He kept his head down, wore T-shirts and jeans, was driven around in a beater of an automobile. He kept no particular residence. He didn't even have his own clothes closet. He stayed different nights at his motel or at the cribs of his different baby mommas. He'd wake up in the morning and put on whatever new clothes his women had bought for him while they were out spending his money on themselves and his kids. (Ross spent a lot of time with his kids when they were young, running and working out, teaching them all to play tennis; several of his sons would end up joining the gang life and running afoul of the law; his eldest daughter works at a CVS drug store.)

As he does today, Ross spent most of his time in a car, riding back and forth on the 110 Freeway and the other massive concrete roadbeds that crisscross the inland empire, checking on his different operations—if ever a childhood nickname grew up with the man, it was his. For a long time, the Freeway Rick Task Force—a squad of hardened drug cops from the L.A. County Sheriff's Department dedicated to his capture—actually had no idea what he looked like. On several occasions Ross walked away from police operations planned for the express purpose of capturing him—since an early age, he'd been known for his quickness, both on the tennis court and also down a dark alley and over a fence.

In 1988, a load of coke bound for his lucrative new territory in Cincinnati was detected by a drug-sniffing dog at a bus station in New Mexico. The drugs were traced to Ross; he was arrested. Federal indictments in Cincinnati, Los Angeles, and Tyler, Texas, were handed down. Ross pleaded guilty to cocaine-trafficking charges and received a mandatory ten-year prison sentence, which he began serving in 1990.

Around this time, a federal investigation into the sheriff's office was uncovering massive corruption. Dozens of narcotics officers were convicted of beating suspects, stealing drug money, and planting evidence. Ross testified for the government. In return he served only four years and nine months of his sentence.

Back home at thirty-four, Rick got a job hauling trash. His major efforts were devoted to an old theater in South Central he wanted to convert into a youth center/recording studio/performance space. While he'd been away in prison, holding on to the theater and his other remaining assets had been costing him nearly fifteen grand a month. With all the money spent on lawyers for himself and his workers, he was nearly broke. He'd paid the owner of the theater $900,000 up front and $6,000 a month while incarcerated. Now Ross was behind in the payments; the owner was threatening to foreclose. Everything else was gone. Ross was determined not to lose the theater, too.

As it happened, right about this time, Ross received a call from his old business partner, Blandón.

In late 1990 or '91, Blandón was arrested by the LAPD with a suitcase full of cash—only to be bailed out by the U. S. Justice Department, which said he was part of a money-laundering case. Then Blandón was arrested by the DEA for conspiracy to distribute cocaine.

While probation officers recommended a life sentence and a $4 million fine, the prosecution argued that Blandón was "extraordinarily valuable in major DEA investigations of Class I drug traffickers," and recommended forty-eight months and no fine. Less than a year later Blandón was freed. In a memo to a judge, the prosecutor wrote that Blandón had "almost unlimited potential to assist the United States... as a full-time, paid informant after his release from prison."

Ross was a little surprised to hear from Blandón, but they'd always done beautiful business together. Ross and a friend drove to Blandón's downtown L.A. restaurant. After they chatted and caught up, Blandón got to his point. "The Colombians are on my back," he told Ross. He owed money; he had a shipment he needed to sell. "Why go around begging all these people for money for your theater when you can make it all at once?" Blandón asked.

Reluctantly or not, Ross found a buyer; as middleman, he was to receive a commission of $300,000 on a hundred-kilo sale. The deal went down in a shopping-center parking lot near San Diego on March 2, 1995. The DEA and local authorities swooped in. Ross's arrest netted Blandón more than $45,000 in government rewards and reimbursements. Ross was found guilty of conspiring to sell cocaine that had been provided by the DEA, in a deal set up by the DEA, a typical drug-war scenario. Ross received what was identified as his third felony strike, and with it a sentence of life in prison without possibility of parole.

Over the next few years Ross, who had learned to read only during his first stretch in jail, painstakingly read every business and self-help book in the prison library—during a fourteen-year period, he boasts, he devoured more than three hundred books. His trilogy of favorites: *Think and Grow Rich,* by Andrew Carnegie disciple Napoleon Hill; *The Richest Man in Babylon,* by George Samuel Clason; and *As a Man Thinketh,* by James Allen. Eventually, Ross held study groups with other inmates, spreading the word of economic self-sufficiency and can-do capitalism among the brothers. If we can be so successful selling crack, Ross preached, why can't we use the same skills toward legitimate business?

In late 1995, inmate 05550-045 was visited by journalist Gary Webb. Webb's *Mercury News* series, "Dark Alliance," was published in August 1996, and later became a book. Webb charged that the U. S. government had secretly allowed shipments of cocaine into the country in order to finance the purchase of weapons needed for the contra rebels to fight the leftist Sandinistas who'd taken over Nicaragua. Ross was portrayed as an unwitting pawn in a game of international covert politics.

After leaving his job in disgrace and watching his marriage dissolve, Webb methodically sold off his possessions and committed suicide in December 2004. According to the coroner's report, on his first attempt to shoot himself in the head, the father of three children missed the mark—instead he suffered a nonfatal wound. He placed the muzzle of his .38-caliber pistol against his head a second time and pulled the trigger.

Meanwhile, Ross sued, asking for more than $5 million in damages from the government. Although his case was rejected, his profile was raised mightily in a black community that had seized upon the notion that a government conspiracy was to blame for the plague of crack. In the people's mythology, the kingpin had become the victim, an antihero and a martyr.

Stuck in prison with a life sentence, Ross "started consuming myself with reading law books," he says. "I started reading them the same way I'd sold drugs. When the library opened every morning, I was there standing in line. If I missed lunch, I missed lunch. I would take all of the money I could muster up and make copies of the law books because they wouldn't let us take them back to our cells."

One day Ross found what he thought he was looking for. He'd received the life sentence for being convicted of a third federal crime—his third strike. But technically, he believed, he had only two strikes. Since his charges from the Texas and Ohio convictions had arisen from the commission of the same federal crime, how could they account for two separate strikes?

Excited, Ross called his lawyer, who shot him down. Ross got a court-appointed attorney. In 1998, the Ninth Circuit Court of Appeals agreed with Ross's jailhouse interpretation of the law. Ross's life sentence was reduced to twenty years. He ended up serving fourteen.

On May 4, 2009, he walked out of Texarkana prison into the arms of his woman, Sergeant Mychosia Nightingale. She'd seen Ross on a documentary about crack; she'd written, he'd urged her to read his favorite books. Facing a fourth deployment to Iraq, Nightingale quit the Army and drove from Georgia to Texarkana to pick him up. She spent the week sleeping in her SUV, waiting for him with a duffel bag of new clothes. Today they have two toddlers. He's already teaching them how to swing a tennis racket.

* * *

The real Rick Ross, Freeway Rick Ross, is southbound on the 110 toward home—this time he's riding behind the driver of a gleaming white Escalade limo provided by the producers of *Brand X*, wearing a custom REAL RICK polo shirt that his silk-screener had made up special for his appearance on national TV.

Though Ross had fretted the entire day over the producer's request that he cook crack on TV—eager to please, he'd reluctantly given the caller a list of ingredients, including a Bunsen burner and procaine, an anesthetic that in his experience would cook up very much like crack—Russell Brand never asked him to do so. Instead Ross was trotted out before the studio audience like an old prizefighter and heralded as the "Donald Trump of crack." Though it's not what Ross was looking for—to be at once lionized and lampooned—it is probably a decent characterization. At the end of the segment, Brand could be heard blurting out something about cooking crack on national television; clearly, cooler heads had prevailed on this last episode before cancellation.

"All these interviews I do every day, all the meetings I take, all the hands I shake, all the pictures, hopefully it amounts to stuff," Ross says, slouching deeply in the seat of the Escalade limo, reflecting on the day's events. He sounds a little tired. It is nearly midnight, another long day.

"I just have to keep pressing and pressing and, you know, fight through all the little things. In the drug business I became an expert at drugs. I knew who sold drugs in Compton, in Watts, on the West Side, in the Jungle. And everybody knew me. But when it comes to Hollywood and this other stuff, I don't know it yet. It's like that Hollywood producer. After that long meeting and we was leaving, he laughed and he said to everybody, 'Why am I shaking hands with this drug dealer?'"

Outside Ross's window, a police cruiser pulls even with the Escalade. The cop riding shotgun appears to be pointing at Ross, though this is impossible, given the fancy blacked-out windows in the limo. Ross has a recurring dream in which he's asleep in one of his old rock houses and a battering ram is knocking down the wall. He still wakes up sometimes not knowing where he is—twenty of his fifty-three years have been spent in cells in different facilities. He knows he's lucky he's not still behind bars.

Ross gestures toward the cops. "Don't you wanna know what they're thinking?"

"You don't have to worry about what they're thinking," I tell him.

"Not no more. Not like I used to," he says. In a month's time, he'll finally land a deal for a miniseries about his life—not the deal he wanted, but at least *something* he believes will pay off. He smiles big and his eyes bug gleefully, a little bit proud of himself. "I ain't going to jail tonight."

Smoking: A Love Story

Okay, okay, okay.

All right already.

I admit: I have a cough.

It's a tiny little cough, neither acute nor chronic. *Recurring* would probably describe it best, be most accurate. In the morning it is dry. During the day it goes away. In the evening it returns, slightly productive. A little cough, okay? A smoker's cough.

The last time I played one-on-one, I saw stars after five points. I get winded when I mess around with my kid, when I mess around with my wife. The kid is three. The marriage is six. I shouldn't be that whipped. Now and then, my heart evinces a random ping, an odd pang, a curious, fluttery loop-de-loop. I've spent long, fretful minutes contemplating the involuntary mechanics of my heart and lungs, monitoring the rise and fall of my chest, listening to the secret sounds within, envisioning all manner of ironic, early demise. By the end of the day, my chest feels thick, woolen, scratchy. If I laugh with gusto, it backs down into a wheeze. I get these pains. They have to do with my spine, sitting and typing, avoiding strenuous exercise, any exercise at all. It feels as if I have a broken rib. As if I can't get enough air. As if it has to do with my lungs.

My grandmother died of lung cancer. She was eighty-seven. I am forty-one. I should live so long. In my memory, she is never without a cigarette—a Benson & Hedges 100—dangling from the left corner of her mouth, one eye scrunched against the spiral of rising smoke, tiny cylinders of ash falling to the carpet, leaving a trail across the linoleum, a secret path to a hidden compartment of her soul, a tiny oasis of perverse nonconformity that lived within her otherwise textbook character, this four-and-a-half-foot Jewish *bubbe* from downtown Baltimore, with beauty-shop hair and oversize blue bifocals. The odd thing about Grandma's smoking was the way she inhaled—she didn't. Sometimes, she'd take a brief puff, blow a hurried cloud into the air. But usually, she just let it dangle there, smoldering. Probably killed herself with her own secondhand smoke.

Secondhand smoke. There's a good one. Authoritative figures released periodically by the government—death by cigarette across a room. Who comes up with this stuff? That's what I want to know. Grandma, I'll give you. The source of her disease was pretty obvious if you accept that smoking cigarettes can lead to lung cancer, which I guess I do, even though I also have a feeling that genetics plays the major part, that if you're predisposed to cancer, you'll get it, no matter how many bran muffins you eat. What I really have a problem with is the notion that all these people are killed each year by passive smoke—forty thousand a year, according to the last published reports. What are the scientific controls in this counting? How do they diagnose the victims? What about the air? Item from a sports-medicine newsletter: A half-hour jog on a smoggy day causes lung damage equivalent to that of smoking a pack of cigarettes. Item from Gannett News Service: The leading cause of death in the world is acute respiratory infection spread by airborne bacteria and viruses. Item from the AP: Releases of greenhouse gases by U. S. industry rose more than 3.5 percent in 1996, compared with a total 8 percent growth during the preceding six years. Items from CNN: Indonesian fires, Caribbean volcanoes, Eastern-bloc radioactivity, African disease, American consumption of gasoline at an all-time high.

Secondhand smoke. You don't have to be Ralph Nader to know that we are killing ourselves with sport-utes and WebTVs, with electromagnets and microwave transmitters, and that we are blaming it all on Joe Camel. They couldn't win the war on drugs, so they made cigarettes a drug and declared war on them. Drug Delivery Device. Brilliant Political Ploy: control something you already control. Blur the issues. Identify a scapegoat. Rally the citizens. Encourage them to quit smoking. Encourage them to jog fifteen minutes every day behind a bus. Run For Your Life. You better believe it.

Okay, okay, okay.

All right already.

I admit: I am afraid.

Afraid to die. This image I have: lying in a motorized hospital bed in the living room of my dream house, tubes protruding, an oxygen mask, my wife and son sitting one on each side, frightened, holding my hands, avoiding my eyes.

Afraid to stop smoking. This image I have: standing in a huge crowd, just another one of the assholes, another penitent, confused, judgmental, gullible follower, nodding my head, toeing the line, counting calories, counting grams of fat, counting heartbeats with a crook-wristed hand resting Jack Benny-like on the artery in my neck, climbing stairs and riding bikes that go nowhere, walking on a treadmill, for chrissakes (talk about your ugly metaphors), another smug, pitiful, politically correct nonsmoker squinting and grimacing and wrinkling my nose, dismissing the noxious fumes that I loved so well with a series of fey, intolerant little waves—just another hypocrite with a constant guilty craving for a cigarette.

* * *

I don't feel so good. I have never written a word for publication without a cigarette burning in the ashtray. It's a synergistic thing, this process, typing, a manic internal flight across an obstacle course in the desert, jumping moguls and skirting rocks, churning up dirt and dust, thoughts firing like spark plugs in a four-stroke motocross engine, the energy converted by synaptic pistons into touch-type muscle memory, fingers pumping, dancing, tickling the keys like ivories, like the head of a table drum, *tinka tinka tink tonk,* mumbling the words out loud, breathing on the commas, a vague, contrapuntal song droning under the percussive rhythm of the keyboard, a low moan, something like Oscar Peterson playing a solo, eyes glued to the screen, the letters appearing serendipitously, marching across the page. Pause a moment. Reread. Right hand working the cursor. Left hand reaching for the cigarette burning in the periphery of my vision. Grasp the filter between the thumb and the first two fingers, tap it once with the index, the falling ash, the arc to the lips, the wind over the teeth, the smoke filling the mouth, the tang, a unique flavor, not so much tobacco as something best described as green, a True Green taste, menthol, mint, celery, depending on the time of day and the number already consumed, the lungs full, the tingle, the exhalation, the billowing stream of smoke, carried across the room on invisible currents, mingling with the dust motes in the air, illuminated by a shaft of light. Quitting, they say, makes you lightheaded and unable to focus. It clouds your thinking. This is not the greatest thing for a writer. It's the last excuse I have. What if I can't write anymore?

What if I die of lung disease and I can't write anymore?

At the end of this piece, I have resolved, I will quit. I will write these words; I will talk myself down from the ledge. I will type "The End." Then I will throw away my cigarettes. I will become a nonsmoker. I will move on. I don't know yet what I'm going to do with my lighters. The thin-silhouette, brass Civil War reproduction, six dollars at Britches, that took me through college, through my thirties, around the world. The laser-shaped butane torch that took me so many times into the zone. The neat flameless number I use at the beach. The simple, chrome-plated Zippo with its satisfying song, the metallic click and *shick* of the top levered open, the flint wheel spun, given to me by my wife, engraved I LOVE YOU, such a neat object, this inexpensive lighter etched with fancy italic letters, a symbol to me of my wife and her way of getting to the bottom of things, to the heart of meanings, to the heart of me; someone else would have chosen gold and I would have left it in the box. And what of my ashtrays? The hand-painted terra-cotta sun and moon from Positano. The thick, green cylinder of marble from Agra. The large, rectangular ceramic decorated with pink flamingos in a natural blue-and-green setting. The brass Frankart lady standing naked by my favorite chair, holding the heavy amber glass tray above her head in perpetuity just for me. And my volcanoes, those great little Japanese devices that sit inside the ashtrays. A wonderful invention, simple and brilliant, some made of fired clay to look like their namesake, some made of industrial alloy, pentagonal-shaped, inch-deep machine bolts. You place the lit cigarette in the hole in the top, a simple male-to-female action, and your cigarette goes out immediately. No scraping or tapping, no burning of the fingers, no smoldering, just out, dead, over. These are my things. My particular, peculiar, personal things. The contents of my baggage. What am I to do with them? I can't just throw them away. Storage, I guess, as soon as I finish this piece, my little conversation with myself, my little pep talk, my lecture, my eulogy to smoke and the smoking life, my love sonnet—"Ode to a Carolina Cigarette," "Romeo and Nicotine." Currently, I am at the bottom of page five. I have been writing for more than a week. This is not fast for me. There is no carrot at the end of this stick, nothing immediate to urge me on. Only the vague hope that once I quit, I will start putting time back on the clock, I will live a little longer. And the vague dread that tomorrow I'll be hit by a truck.

On my desk is a box of patches, a nicotine transdermal system, step one, twenty-one milligrams. I've used something similar before, the nicotine gum, though not exactly in the manner intended. One piece every two hours on a long airline flight and I am much less inclined to kill the flight attendant when she puts her hands on my seat and forces me into an upright position for landing. The gum, of course, was a Band-Aid solution, temporary, rather clever, a thumb to the notion of the pious national zeal for quitting, for making it tough on smokers, for punishing us, for relieving us of our rights in the name of the public good. No smoking? I'll show you, you guilt-filled yuppie sheep, you clueless legislators of public morality! Chew on this, fuckers: nicotine gum!

These patches, however, are something altogether different. You wear them for twenty-four hours. You can't alternate them with cigarettes. Forgetting for a moment the amusing notion that to use them I must find seven separate places on my body that have no hair, these patches are serious: a permanent solution, radical surgery, amputation. The cigarette will henceforth be gone from my hands, from my ashtrays, from my persona. The patches are to be used in graduated doses over ten weeks. The instruction booklet warns of the possibility of "vivid" dreams, sleeplessness, irritability. I might get headaches, feel dizzy and a little out of sorts, feel sweaty, or have stomach upsets. These are typical nicotine-withdrawal symptoms, the booklet says. They will go away with time. In Israel, they cure people of heroin dependence by putting them to sleep until the symptoms subside. It seems like a much better plan.

This brand, NicoDerm CQ, was advertised especially for people who like a cigarette in the morning. For the last two decades, breakfast has been my favorite meal: coffee and cigarettes—half a pot, three or four. Until a few years ago, the first cigarette was the best of the day. Before I was married, I'd have it in bed. I'd awaken, roll over, light up. No matter that my lungs had felt like an ashtray the night before; the morning was a new lease, the wind bags felt clear. I'd suck in the cool blue smoke, and my eyes would pop. Good morning! All would be right again in my world. Lately, that first cigarette is kind of labored. I want it. I need it. I wake up thinking about it. Then I light it. It makes my chest tight and scratchy. It makes me want to cough. It makes me worry for myself. I smoke it anyway.

My wife brought the patches home ten days ago at my request. I have to give her credit. She has never nagged. She has never said a word. Well, the other night, she asked if I'd been coughing a lot lately I answered yes. Then I lit another cigarette. That commercial in which the woman smokes through the surgical hole in her neck? That makes me want to smoke, too. When my wife put the patches on the table, a neutral gesture, just the simple placement of an object she'd purchased on my behalf, I began to cry. It was a short cry, more of a sob, really, one of those heaves, a spontaneous emotional hiccup that forced a solitary tear from my eye. It ran down my cheek, lost itself in my beard. Later that night, as I watched *Doug*, the children's cartoon, it happened again. I feel raw and unstable right now, quite out of sorts. Like someone has died. Like someone is about to die. A fond old friend, my beloved habit.

Also on my desk is a carton of cigarettes. I think I'll have another one now. My current orders to myself: Fire at will. Burn, baby, burn. I am on page seven, week two, carton two, of writing my way to better health. It is 10:55 A.M. I began typing this morning at 8:30. There are eight dead cigarettes in the sun-and-moon ashtray, littered about like pickup sticks on a bed of dark, dry ash, each smoked to within a half inch of the filter, each ulcered with burns from subsequent numbers that were lit, sucked, balanced in the tray, volcanoed. I am picking up speed. A few more days and I will be finished.

I rattle the pack, and another True Green mambos out of the foil liner. True Menthol King Size. Tasteful ultralow tar, unique plastic flavor-chamber filter. A silver-and-green package—updated some years ago from white and green; that alone a shock to the system, like coming home one day and finding that your wife has unexpectedly dyed her hair. Surgeon general's warning: QUITTING SMOKING NOW GREATLY REDUCES SERIOUS RISKS TO YOUR HEALTH.

In high school photography, I once did a still life with packages of True. There was something then and now very Jenny Holzer about my chosen brand, an odd brand, I admit, but I am loyal. It's True, man. What more need be said? My mother smoked True Greens. I guess Freud would have had fun with that. My father smoked True Blues—probably significant as well. Given those facts, you could extrapolate that I've been exposed to True Greens since the moment of my conception, or, more accurately perhaps, since the moment directly thereafter, when my mom rolled over and lit one up, a personal environmental constant no doubt written into the puzzle of my DNA—a companion, a security blanket, a set of worry beads, a recurring prop in the movie of my life:

Nine years old in the driveway, behind the wheel of the family Corvair. A crooked, half-smoked True Green butt with lipstick on the filter. The electric metal taste of tobacco ignited by the glowing coil. The neighbor girl, watching from the edge of her yard. My first drag. My first kiss. Thirteen: miniature hippie. Hair trying to get long, keep-on-truckin' boots, legs crossed Indian style on the floor, rocking back and forth autistically to the feedback and the blues groove at the drop-in teen center, trying to act stoned, smoking a True Green. Fifteen: first postcoital True Green. Málaga, Spain. Four thousand air miles to sleep with a girl in hip-hugger peanut jeans and a midriff blouse who lived seven miles across my hometown. Eighteen: a ten-flat, hundred-yard dash, one of three freshmen on varsity soccer. Daily ten-mile runs, followed by a bong hit and a True Green. Twenty: chest hair, gold chain, professional goals, prelaw. Do your own thing but have a degree to fall back on. Coffee and True Greens at the student union. Twenty-two: cocaine and True Greens at four in the morning in the basement press office at police headquarters. Twenty-seven: Thomas the pimp and his girl bumming True Greens on the whore stroll, ten blocks from the White House. Thirty: True Greens and salted, buttery tea in a Buddhist monastery in the north of Nepal, a monk in the corner of the room levitating three inches off the ground. Thirty-three: True Greens and super-freak—silk ropes, battery-operated accessories, a crack cook-off with a female lawyer in a tenement apartment on the Lower East Side. Thirty-five: True Greens and marriage vows, wedding night. Thirty-eight: True Greens in the courtyard outside the hospital, waiting for my son to be born.

Now forty-one: True Greens and quitting. True Greens and the fear of death.

Lever the helmet of the Zippo, the familiar ringing metallic click, spin the flint wheel, *shick*, the spark, the fluttering blue-and-orange spirit of the flame, inhale, exhale, thick, cloudy stream. There has always been this part of me, this smoker, living deep and root-bound within my character, a rich vein of recalcitrance, a buried wellspring of perversity, a mulish, self-righteous desire to do things my own way, determine my own fate, think for myself. The authorities say quit, and that makes me want to smoke. Question authority, they used to say. I still do.

I hate waiting, craving, wanting; I hate denying myself things. This is what they've been pushing on us for the last decade or so. Just Say No. Why ask why? Denial, in truth, is the source of all evil. As humans, we have our needs; sometimes they aren't very pretty. But if we don't allow ourselves a certain access, the pressure builds; simple desire mutates into dark, complex obsession. Like this guy I know, once a successful adman. Some years back, he found religion, decided he wouldn't have sex again until marriage. Ended up bankrupting himself with crack and hookers. Or the whole cigar vogue, which washed up on the shores of popular culture just about the time when cigarette smoking was banned in most restaurants. Or all those priests being tried for molesting children. Maybe if they were allowed at least to relieve themselves... No pain, I have always believed, simply means no pain. Gain is something else again. Positives are not born from negatives; they are born from positives. My lifelong motto: I want to do what I want to do. It's not that I'm spoiled. I don't mean anyone any harm. Just give me my options and read me your concerns. Let me figure it out for myself.

Now what I've figured out, I guess, is that I want to quit smoking. Well, I don't really want to quit, but I have admitted to myself that I have a cough, that I get winded, that I have these pains, that I don't want to die before my time because two very special people really need me. Some years ago, before they started the bit with the secondhand smoke, they were running a public-service commercial that said each cigarette takes six minutes off your life. If you forget for a moment the dubious source and scientific value of the figure—forget for a moment that this was another decade's version of authoritative information released by some secret propaganda mill buried deep within the murky catacombs of the government colony of ants—that's what this is all about, time off my life, the fear of death, the reaching of that certain milestone, that certain age when you see not just the future anymore but also the end. Forty-one years old, regular smoker since eighteen, conservatively twenty-five cigarettes a day. That's 209,875 cigarettes. Six minutes off my life for each one: 874 days.

Wait a minute. That's only, what, a little more than two years. Better check the math.

That's right, 874. Hmmm.

So only two years and a little off my life. Say I live to be eighty instead of eighty-two. Two fewer years of drooling. What do I care? My wife will be seventy. She'll be ready to be rid of me by then, I'm sure. The kid will be forty-three. Shit, older than I am right now. He'll be all right. I mean, you don't want to lose your dad, but at that age you're pretty much on your own, anyway. Hopefully, I'll have some money to leave him. Might even get to see my own grandkid.

Excuse me a minute. I'm going to go talk to my wife.

* * *

It is three days later now, page twelve. I've broken the three-week mark on writing. I've finished huge narrative investigations in less time. I've also broken the carton of cigarettes, just opened the last pack.

When I went upstairs to tell my wife about the math, she kind of lost that cool I was talking about earlier. "Only two years?" she repeated sarcastically. "What if that means two years before

Miles's bar mitzvah? Or two years before his high school graduation? Or two years before his own son is born? Or two years before you finish your precious novel?

"And what if that two years is preceded by ten years on an oxygen tank? I'm not going to carry you down the steps to your office every morning. And if you can't work, we won't be able to afford someone to carry you down there, either. You think it's dramatic releasing your book posthumously? Good for sales, right? You're gonna want to see it on the best-seller list, aren't you? You think you'll even have the energy to type on your beloved computer? You think you'll have the energy to wipe your own ass? Enough already, Mike. Get a clue. This charade has gone on long enough. You must have written a book down there already. Finish. Move on. It is time to quit."

By the time we'd finished our little talk, it was late in the day, time for me to see my new chiropractor, who had told me that those pains in my ribs were due to subluxations in my spine, that a little adjusting and a little exercise would set me straight. It was a good treatment, I thought, the resounding cracks in my back producing the same giddy sense of accomplishment as does the successful milking of a ripe pimple, The treatment was followed by my first therapeutic massage, complete with dim light and oils and new-age music, a petite female masseuse with running shoes and very firm thighs, whose soft, effortful breathing behind my car reminded me of sex.

The next morning, Saturday, I woke up to take my wife and son to the airport. As I rose, I felt a slight tenderness in my right testicle and a pretty strong pain in the lower right side of my back. Being that it was five in the morning and they had to catch a plane for the East Coast, I didn't pay the pains much mind. By the time I got home, the testicle was noticeably swollen, and it was hard to walk. Late that afternoon, I called the chiropractor. He was a little baffled by the events, though it was possible, he said, that the adjustment could have caused some pain in the internal organs, the nerves being connected to the spine as they are. He suggested that I go to the emergency room. I demurred.

By evening, I had a fever, just over 100. I called the urologist. His partner, whom I've never met, was on duty. After a tense hour, he returned the call. He said it sounded as if I had epididymitis, an inflammation of the chord leading to the testicle. He prescribed some antibiotics and said if it got bad, I could go to the emergency room. Otherwise, I should call my doctor Monday and try to get an appointment during regular office hours.

By Sunday, I was immobile and in great pain. I lay on the couch, watching football. I was hungry, but I couldn't really walk, and I wasn't going to drive anywhere. The pain in the testicle had radiated upward into my abdomen. The pain in my back had radiated downward into my right leg. I thought about calling one of the neighbors, but I'm new here and didn't really want to discuss my right testicle with either Joe and Pearl or Warren and Betty, the lovely seniors who live on either side, all of whom have worse medical problems of their own, I am sure. By Sunday night, my fever had reached 101. I considered going to the emergency room, but I am a doctor's son. The ER is for gunshots and broken bones and heart attacks, not prickly medical mysteries. I decided to gut it out.

As the night progressed, I had visions of my scrotum exploding. I wondered if maybe I was bleeding internally. I wondered if the chiropractor had somehow cut off circulation to my testicle. I envisioned gangrene, amputation, even the follow-up cosmetic surgery, the placement of a prosthetic ball. Settling into bed, I actually wondered if I'd wake up the next day.

Now it is Tuesday. I went to the doctor yesterday, a heroic effort of fear over pain, and he diagnosed epididymitis. Where it came from he could not say. Just another riddle of health and science to be treated with pills and further tests.

I want to do what I want to do. Yeah, right. Tell it to my testicle. Tell it to my spine. Tell it to my lungs. We are helpless in the face of infirmity, helpless against the serendipitous onset of pain and disease and infection and death, helpless against a medical system in which doctors don't find it worth their while to involve themselves personally with treatment on the weekends. You might try to live your life according to your own smug, personal constellation of reality, but the body, it seems, has a reality of its own, and the truth of the matter is, my fear of sickness is even greater than my fear of death.

There is no control in sickness. You can't do what you want to do. You can't do shit but ail, lie there like a weepy child, quiet and passive, praying to the greater spirits that you get better, not worse. Forget about the government, the hypocrites. Forget about the image, the persona. Forget about the recurring prop in the movie of my life. The fact is, I have a cough, I get winded, I have these pains. My body has put me on notice, has issued a warning. It is an authority not to be questioned.

Okay, okay, okay.

All right already.

The End.

I quit.

Sources

When Should a Man Stop Smoking Weed? – *Playboy* – September, 2013

Dab Artists – *The California Sunday Magazine* – May 3, 2015

The Rise and Fall of a Super Freak – A version of this story first appeared in *Rolling Stone* – 1996

Generation H – A version of this story first appeared in *GQ* – September, 1995

The Teachings of Don Carlos – *Scary Monsters and Super Freaks: Stories of Sex, Drugs, Rock 'N' Roll and Murder* (Da Capo Press)

Death in Venice – A version of this story first appeared in *Rolling Stone* – September, 1994

The High Life and Strange Times of the Pope of Pot – *Rolling Stone* – June, 1991

The Real Rick Ross is Not a Rapper – A version of this story first appeared in *Esquire* – September, 2013

Smoking: A Love Story – *Esquire* – February, 1998

About the Author

Mike Sager is a best-selling author and award-winning reporter. A former Washington Post staff writer under Watergate investigator Bob Woodward, he worked closely, during his years as a contributing editor to *Rolling Stone*, with gonzo journalist Hunter S. Thompson. Sager is the author of 6 collections of non-fiction, two novels, and one biography. He has served for more than eighteen years as a writer at large for Esquire. In 2010 he won the National Magazine Award for profile writing. Many of his stories have been optioned for film. For more information, please see www.MikeSager.com.

About the Publisher

The Sager Group was founded in 1984. In 2012 it was chartered as a multi-media artists' and writers' consortium, with the intent of empowering those who make art—an umbrella beneath which makers can pursue, and profit from, their craft directly, without gatekeepers.

TSG publishes eBooks and paper books; manages musical acts and produces live shows; ministers to artists and provides modest grants; and produces documentary, feature and web-based films. By harnessing the means of production, The Sager Group helps artists help themselves. For more information, please see www.TheSagerGroup.Net.

Other Books by Mike Sager

High Tolerance, A Novel

The Someone You're Not

Scary Monsters and Super Freaks

Revenge of the Donut Boys

Wounded Warriors

Deviant Behavior, A Novel

The Devil and John Holmes

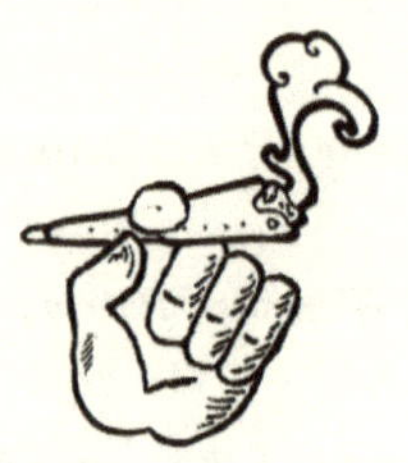

www.ingramcontent.com/pod-product-compliance
Lightning Source LLC
Chambersburg PA
CBHW050317110726
47899CB00007B/2275

* 9 7 8 0 9 8 6 2 6 7 9 7 0 *